City and Power – Postmodern Urban Spaces in Contemporary Poland

WARSAW STUDIES IN PHILOSOPHY AND SOCIAL SCIENCES

Edited by
Tadeusz Szawiel and Jakub Kloc-Konkołowicz

VOLUME 8

PETER LANG

Katarzyna Kajdanek/Igor Pietraszewski/Jacek Pluta (eds.)

City and Power –
Postmodern Urban Spaces in
Contemporary Poland

PETER LANG

Bibliographic Information published by the Deutsche Nationalbibliothek
The Deutsche Nationalbibliothek lists this publication in the Deutsche
Nationalbibliografie; detailed bibliographic data is available in the
internet at http://dnb.d-nb.de.

Library of Congress Cataloging-in-Publication Data
Names: Kajdanek, Katarzyna, 1981- editor. | Pietraszewski, Igor, 1962-editor. | Pluta,
Jacek, 1971 - editor.
Title: City and power : postmodern urban spaces in contemporary Poland / Katarzy-
na Kajdanek, Igor Pietraszewski, Jacek Pluta (eds.).
Description: New York : Peter Lang, [2017] | Series: Warsaw studies in philosophy and
social sciences ; Vol. 8 | Includes bibliographical references.
Identifiers: LCCN 2017026538| ISBN 9783631664902 (Print : alk. paper) | ISBN
9783653057416 (E-PDF) | ISBN 9783631705773 (EPUB) | ISBN 9783631705780 (MOBI)
Subjects: LCSH: Urban renewal--Poland--Wroclaw. | Wroclaw (Poland)--Buildings,
structures, etc. | Sociology, Urban--Poland--Wroclaw. | Wroclaw
(Poland)--History--21st century.
Classification: LCC HT178.P6 C58 2017 | DDC 307.3/4160943852--dc23 LC record
available at https://lccn.loc.gov/2017026538

This publication was financially supported by the University of Wroclaw.

ISSN 2196-0143
ISBN 978-3-631-66490-2 (Print)
E-ISBN 978-3-653-05741-6 (E-PDF)
E-ISBN 978-3-631-70577-3 (EPUB)
E-ISBN 978-3-631-70578-0 (MOBI)
DOI 10.3726/978-3-653-05741-6

© Peter Lang GmbH
Internationaler Verlag der Wissenschaften
Berlin 2018
All rights reserved.

Peter Lang – Berlin · Bern · Bruxelles · New York ·
Oxford · Warszawa · Wien

This publication has been peer reviewed.

www.peterlang.com

Contents

Katarzyna Kajdanek, Jacek Pluta & Igor Pietraszewski

Preface: Wrocław, a City of Success?

The idea of writing an anthology of texts devoted to Wrocław – a large city in south-west Poland – emerged as a result of a longer process. Its main subject – the nature of social transition in Poland from the perspective of local politics – stemmed from observations of urban movements that are now on the increase. By positioning themselves in opposition to the local government, urban movements have become an important player in the local public sphere. The local government elections in 2014, in which urban movements in Poland achieved the best results in their history, demonstrated the political significance of this process. In many big cities, long-standing mayors lost or, as in Wrocław, won only in the second ballot and with great difficulty[1]. This situation was only partly rooted in voter apathy and a jaded approach from the incumbents. Most of all, it was related to the dynamic of the social changes that accompany the current Polish political transition.

In the initial period of the transition (from 1989 to the beginning of the 21st century) the most crucial problems for the authorities were related to the construction of a new political, economic and social order. Solving these problems was necessary to overcome developmental delays. On a local level, it was necessary to establish democratic rules in the form of self-government. It is important to note that the construction of self-governmental order in Poland was clearly divided into two stages. The first stage began in 1990, when territorial self-government was restored at gmina (municipality) level. The second level of local and regional self-government (counties, Polish: powiat) with both self-governing bodies and a structure representing the state administration (voivodships, Polish: województwo) was established in 1998 and became operational as of 1 January 1999. Between 1989 and 2004 the narrative about Polish towns and their problems focused on economic transition, particularly the shift from an industrial to a service sector, as well as social problems such as unemployment. This narrative was accompanied by a quite universal political discourse that referred to historical heritage, which was related to the need to build an attractive image of Polish cities in Europe. However, somewhere around 2014, a change could be observed in these narratives. Problems

---

1   In the local government elections in 2010, 25 of 107 Polish mayors were elected in the first ballot; in 2014, as many as 41 (https://pl.wikipedia.org/wiki/Prezydenci_miast_w_Polsce_(kadencja_2014–2018).

related to the political, economic and social transition were gradually giving way to new challenges, rooted in global economic processes and cultural changes.

The processes of reflective monitoring of the public sphere were gradually forcing the local authorities to modify their narrative. This alteration can be described as the change of *the political*,[2] i.e. a narrative method that introduces locality in place of statehood. At first glance, this change seemed attractive to local politicians who like to emphasise the increasing role of cities and their autonomy in a globalised world. On the other hand, the discussed changes may also be unfavourable to the local authorities, as the reflexivity of the public sphere undermines their authority and their narrative. As a result, the public sphere is revitalised as a space of articulation for local advocacy groups who object to the narrative and activities of the authorities. All these phenomena display the changing rules of the public sphere: a process in which power is being gradually distributed among different actors of the public sphere.

This book discusses events that are direct or indirect examples of *the political* in the urban public sphere; they involve relations between the local authorities, other local actors and the ordinary citizens. To offer a broader context for these analyses, we will now provide a short profile of Wrocław.

Wrocław, a city with a population of 636,000, has been undergoing a process of transition since 1989 that is typical for all cities in Poland, that is, from a socialist city characterised by:

- no self-government on a local level;
- a limited urban public sphere, controlled by the central government;
- limited economy based on industrial production;
- dysfunctional and often degraded public space, unsuited to citizens' requirements concerning the quality of life;

to a post-industrial city, in which:

- local governments are autonomous from the central government;
- in addition to production, consumption has an important role in the city's economy; as a result, the urban system of opportunities and satisfaction of needs develops, particularly in the sphere of leisure;
- the logic of growth is increasingly based on competition for resources on a national and global level;

---

2   We do not define the political in terms of conflicts in the public sphere, after C. Schmidt or Ch. Mouffe (2005) but rather in T. Parson's theoretical framework, as a generalised quality of the public sphere that influences the actions of its actors (motives, mode of action, narratives, etc.).

- with the increasing potential for development of urban advocacy groups, the importance of quality of life issues related to urban resources is also growing;
- the public sphere becomes important as a moderator of urban life.

The post-Fordist model of urban development in developed countries, widely discussed by researchers, emphasised that cities are subject to macrostructural conditions (Błaszczyk 2015; Castells 1989, 2011), which leads to predictable and inevitable consequences (demographic, economic, social and cultural). On the other hand, many researchers share a view that postmodern cities are important centres for moderating social-economic processes, which, when used by local politicians and businesses, can bring them considerable profits (Florida 2005). However, there are also critical voices about negative consequences of development processes in cities that are based on unsustainable consumption (Zukin 1993, 1998, 2003; Clark et. al. 2003), financial speculation and domination of neoliberal ideology, which lead to social destruction (Harvey 2008).

Regardless of the debate about the uncertain future of cities, in the case of Wrocław the consequences of changes seem positive. For example, Wrocław was ranked 87th of 141 world cities in Mercer's Quality of Life Index 2016 Mid-Year, ahead of Milan (88th), Saint Petersburg (119th) or Beijing (128th) and with only two Polish cities ahead of it: Warsaw (72nd) and Cracow (84th).[3]

Thanks to a positive net internal migration rate, the population in Wrocław remains constant despite the negative demographic processes observed in other Polish cities. Over the past years, unemployment has significantly decreased and it is now below 3%, making the city an attractive labour market in the region as well as on a national scale. A new phenomenon is a mass influx of migrants from Ukraine. In 2006, 38,000 work permits were issued (Karabon and Karabon 2016: 4). The majority of employees work in the following sectors: industry, trade, education, healthcare, administration, science, insurance, information and communication. In 2012, the GDP per capita in Wrocław was equivalent to 155.2% of Poland's average.[4] The GDP growth between 2004 and 2012 in Wrocław was 45%, which was the second best in Poland (after Rzeszów). Poland's big cities average at 34%.[5]

Wrocław's rank depends on the indicators and criteria for measurement. From a demographic perspective, Wrocław is the fourth most populous and the fifth

---

3   https://www.numbeo.com/quality-of-life/rankings.jsp (accessed 1 December 2016)
4   Data from 2012, see Wrocław w liczbach 2015, Urząd statystyczny we Wrocławiu (Statistical Office in Wrocław); available at www.wroclaw.stat.gov.pl
5   Based on the data of GUS: Central Statistical Office of Poland.

largest city in Poland. Its size is similar to Riga, Oslo or Copenhagen. According to a typology based on spatial planning, such as the ESPON project (Possible European Territorial Futures),[6] Wrocław, alongside Cracow, Katowice, Tri-City (Gdańsk, Gdynia, Sopot), Poznań, Łódź and Szczecin, is classified as a Weak MEGA – a city more peripheral than a potential MEGA (large metropolitan centre). GaWC, another ranking that classifies world cities (based on their integration in the global economy), categorises Wrocław alongside 41 other cities (e.g. Lille, The Hague, Nurnberg, Poznań, Bilbao and Dresden) as a "high sufficiency city", i.e. cities that have a sufficient degree of services so as not to be obviously dependent on world cities (Karabon and Karabon 2016: 7).

Table 1: Potential of Polish cities

City	Population (in thousands)*	GDP per capita Poland=100**	Potential for 7 types of capital according to the PwC methodology***[7]
Tri-City (Gdańsk, Gdynia, Sopot)	747	148	103
Bydgoszcz	359	111	81
Białystok	295	98	83
Warsaw	1724	291	136
Lublin	344	115	91
Rzeszów	183	121	94
Cracow	759	155	112
Katowice	304	142	109
Łódź	711	122	85
Wrocław	632	155	114
Poznań	548	196	107
Szczecin	408	118	86

Source: PwC and GUS data from 2012**, 2013*, 2014*** The concept of 7 capitals include the following: human and social capital, culture and image capital, quality of life capital, technical and infrastructure capital, institutional and democratic capital, investment attractiveness capital and sources of finance capital.

---

6 http://www.espon.eu/main/Menu_Projects/Menu_AppliedResearch/06.TerritorialFutures.html (accessed 25 November 2016) The project is based on a foresight approach. It aims at predicting possible futures of European cities and providing information on factors that affect their development opportunities.

7 Wrocław was one of only two cities ranked in the report that steadily developed its capitals, see Wrocław Nadodrzański mikrokosmos musi dalej rosnąć. PwC 2015, p. 7. (http://www.pwc.pl/pl/pdf/miasta/raport-o-metropoliach-wroclaw-2015.pdf)

The nationwide perception of Wrocław as a successful city is related to the so-called Base effect. In 1990, the developmental potential of Wrocław was estimated distinctly lower than that of other Polish cities, e.g. Szczecin, Łódź or Poznań. Today, the situation is quite the opposite. The success of Wrocław is due to the character of the changes the city underwent. Wrocław is perceived by experts as a city that created its image in a most spectacular way. Importantly, on its path to post-transitional revival, Wrocław managed to avoid the Shrinking City phenomenon (Martinez-Fernandez 2012) – a significant population loss that was experienced by Łódź, for instance. Wrocław also expanded its economic base by developing business and consumer services.

This positive image of transition, however, should not obscure the problems Wrocław is facing. They are related to macrostructural as well as local risks. The most crucial are:

- negative demographic processes, including population ageing;
- suburbanisation and urban sprawl (Kajdanek 2012);
- environmental threats (air pollution, heavy car traffic);
- political threats (the influence of unfavourable changes at central government level – desisting from the path of modernisation, increase in isolationist tendencies);
- investment and economic collapse related to political and globalisation risks – a drop in investments subsidised by EU programmes;
- dysfunctional local public sphere – distance between the local authorities and citizens.

These factors are an increasingly important element of a narrative that has a considerable influence on public opinion, which the social study conducted for the design of development strategy for Wrocław 2030 confirms.[8]

To conclude, in the second decade of the 21st century, Wrocław is commonly perceived as a successful city. On the other hand, studies on the strategy for Wrocław 2030 clearly demonstrate that the actions regarded as sufficient by the authorities show a decreasing level of respect for the citizens' interests. How is this possible?

Local politics in Poland is in many respects the opposite of politics on a central level. It is characterised by structural (financial, political, social) autonomy. There

---

8   See J. Pluta, *Prezentacja wyników badań nad założeniami Strategii Wrocław 2030*, http://www.wroclaw.pl/strategia-rozwoju-wroclawia-2030/files/Wroclaw-2030-prezentacja-media-3.pdf

are no limits on the number of terms of office for a mayor. Local government is to a large extent independent from the context of national politics. In contrast to the central government, the distance between politicians and citizens is shorter and their relations are more empowered and direct. Alongside political parties that are governed by pragmatic interests there are other intermediary structures, which are based on values. Therefore, the role of NGOs, the activity of citizens and their social representatives and individual authority of a mayor are more important than membership of a political party.

Although it would seem that there should not be a discrepancy between the local authorities and the citizens, it is still observed. One source of this discrepancy is the stability of power (unlimited number of terms of office), which can lead to failure to recognise citizens' problems. Cultural and social sources of the discussed discrepancy, however, such as different attitudes and values, are even more important. The first Congress of Urban Movements in 2015 proposed a new model for urban development policy based on the Leipzig Charter on Sustainable European Cities. The most highlighted premises were: citizens' right to make decisions on urban matters, urban democracy with social participation as its core, the role of the city budget in improving the citizens' quality of life and the idea of a community: social integration as opposed to marginalisation and social exclusion.[9]

Relating these ideas to the context of the local public sphere and its condition, one may conclude that the premises of the Congress undermine the institutional mechanisms of the local authorities and they redefine the conditions of *the political*. However, it is important to realise that local politics and expectations of them regarding their aims and strategies are not exclusively the domain of the local authorities. They also include the activities and narratives of other collective actors who act in the urban public sphere.

All the discussed processes compound a general picture of the emergence of a new urban public sphere in Poland in the times of the decline in the narrative of transition and the increase in the narrative about a city's residents, identity and future. This picture provides a necessary background to understand the relationship between the authorities and the city and the factors that will influence this relationship in the future. The anthology of texts in this book compose a study of this relationship. It is presented from the perspective of the local authorities and their prerogatives as well as from the perspective of the urban public sphere

---

9   For more conclusions from the congress, see http://kongresruchowmiejskich.pl/tezy-miejskie/

in which these prerogatives are the subject of a critical narrative by other social actors: urban movements and the citizens.

In the first chapter, which opens a discussion about the power-city relationship, Barbara Pabjan analyses power-knowledge in urban politics. Referring to rich literature, particularly to Eric Hobsbawm, Terence Ranger, Michael Schudson, Richard Sennet and John Bodnar (all inspired by Michel Foucault), the author presents an empirically based study of power-knowledge in local politics of memory, including its social reception and the political motives of the Wrocław elite.

Grzegorz Kozdraś reveals another aspect of non-institutional understanding of local power as symbolic violence, which manifests itself in the activity of youth subcultures. His particular subject of examination is the creation of murals and graffiti as a process of social production of space and the broader context for this phenomenon. Hence the major problem analysed by the author is how subcultures participate in the process of building *sites of memory* by their symbolic appropriation of urban space.

"Transformation of Architectural Space in Wrocław" by Iwona Borowik is a study of transformations in the urban space presented in the context of accompanying social changes and illustrated with the examples of several buildings that were fiercely debated among experts and the citizens of Wrocław. An important background used by the author to present ideological and social contexts of the transformation of urban space was the exuberant decade of the 1990s. During this period the logic of transition was flourishing; it permeated the minds of the authorities and investors and it often expressed the aspirations and expectations of the citizens as a contrast to the socialist narrative that had hitherto prevailed.

Katarzyna Kajdanek and Jacek Pluta offer a look at the problem of the exercise of public authority from the perspective of the activity of the Wrocław cycling movement. It is a social action in which the participants clearly and efficiently mark their presence in the public sphere by demonstrating their ability to exercise social pressure on the institutions of authority and, to a considerable extent, by influencing the attitudes of the citizens. The analysis of the emergence of the bicycle movement is thus a good example of creating a new public sphere.

A consumer logic of development, which dominates in European cities, results in an intensified relationship between local authorities and the field of subsidised municipal culture. Igor Pietraszewski discusses the nature of this relationship as a process of the conversion of capitals in the field of cultural production, in which the dominant role is played by the disposers of economic values – politicians and bureaucrats.

Finally, in his analysis of the football paradigm in Wrocław urban policy, Mateusz Błaszczyk depicts the details of a local sport club and the process of its transformation. Sport-related municipal investments, as well as cultural policy, are examples of consumer ideology. From the perspective of the logics of power, this ideology seems imperative in the developmental policy of the city.

We believe that the relationship between cities and power, which is discussed here from several perspectives, provides a good illustration of the cultural and social transformation of Polish cities at the end of the political transition era.

Barbara Pabjan

The Power over Collective Memory

Abstract: The article presents the empirical results of a study of collective memory in Wrocław and discusses collective memory in a theoretical context of cognitive models and ethnic relations. The empirical results strongly suggest that the collective memory shared by cultural elites is conflictual-discursive and symbolic-consensual, while the collective memory of average citizens is conflictual-symbolic and consensual-discursive.

Keywords: *power-knowledge, power and collective memory, politics of memory*

Introduction

Based on an empirical study of the collective memory[1] of Wrocław residents,[2] this chapter addresses the issue of power over collective memory. There is a popular

---

1 The concept of memory I understand as beliefs about the past, and collective memory is collective beliefs about the past. I agree with those who do not see collective memory as a special or new phenomenon, it is just a form of knowledge about the past. I adopt the perspective of sociology of knowledge.

2 I present the empirical data collected mainly through interviews with individuals (face-to-face paper-to-pencil interviews) but also based on qualitative analysis of community activity reflected in the debates in local newspapers.

The data was collected in stages in five different samples:
- a random sample of Wrocław population N=547;
- a quota sample of students (N=329) of selected university faculties (architecture, history, urban studies, German and Jewish history and culture);
- a quota sample of the elites (N=64) of the city, including representatives of the highest levels of city administration, members of the city council, politicians and leaders and members of organisations related to the city (urban planning, architecture, history of the city, museums, etc.) and significant scholars;
- a quota sample of pupils of the majority of Wrocław secondary schools, final year, (N=512).

Data from these samples is presented depending on the question (the frequency of answers in a sample depends on missing values, and usually it varies because only the valid answers are presented). The research was carried out in 2012–2014 as the part of the project with Lund University – The Memory of Vanished Populations. Due to the fact that the students and elite samples are not probability samples, the conclusions have limited coverage. The research project was supported by The Bank of Sweden Tercentenary Foundation.

belief that cultural elites have the greatest influence on shaping collective memory. This issue is examined here along with the assertion that the degree of influence that cultural elites have has been greatly overestimated. The influence of cultural elites on shaping collective memory is limited, due to the complexity of the process that creates a collective memory; this is not a deterministic process. The overall social context, including economics and politics, the media, the structure of society and education levels can all have an impact on collective memory. The influence of the cultural elite is not easy to determine, because it does not come from a homogeneous group of people who communicate with the public using a variety of channels, e.g. through the education system or popular culture. Cultural elites do not always agree among themselves nor do they share a common view of the future. Collective memory can reflect a struggle for power between various factions of elite intellectual and political social groups. Two cognitive memory models, symbolic and discursive, are proposed to explain how collective memory differs among social groups that have gone through either conflictual or consensual ethnic relations.

In the introductory part, the meaning of power-knowledge is discussed and a short overview of the theories of power-knowledge is presented. The main part presents the results of empirical research that were categorised into three groups:

- Local politics of memory, i.e. a typical example of power-knowledge, which includes such phenomena as the creation of commemorative practices and sites of memory, public interpretation of history as well as myths and traditions.
- Power-knowledge as a relation: the structural asymmetry of the statuses of collective memory, the variety of forms of collective memory, the relationship between official and unofficial memory and public and private memory, alternative forms of memory and the tension between official memory and counter-memories. Using two cognitive memory models (symbolic and discursive) I analyse the difference between the memory of the elite and popular memory, which are examples of official and unofficial memory, taking into account their specificity as well as the different interests of the social groups that also determine the content of memory.
- The institutional power over memory: the power of social actors (elites, non-governmental organisations, the media).

What is power and power-knowledge? Terminology problems and the state of research

From a sociological perspective, power is a multidimensional phenomenon that refers to many aspects of social life. Theories of power are very diverse. Some of them focus on violence and coercion, others on normative regulation. Power is associated with the use of force as well as with the ability to influence and impact others. Definitions of power include the actor who exercises power and the object of power; the specific, asymmetric social relationship; the means of exercising control, such as coercion and violence, but also giving rewards. Power is analysed on a micro and macro social level: as an element of culture (e.g. normative power), economy or politics, as a media mechanism, etc.

Similarly to power, the concept of power-knowledge, or the power over memory, is ambiguous. Of many essential factors (coercion, dependence, asymmetry of social relations, violence, sanctions, social norms as the basis for the legitimacy of power), legitimacy and asymmetry of social relations are the most useful in the analysis of power-knowledge. Power as an asymmetric relation resulting from social structures can explain the inequality of resources and influence on collective memory. The specific nature of power-knowledge is that it is based on legitimacy, norms and tradition rather than coercion, violence and sanctions.

This chapter also refers to theories that define power as a possibility of influence on the knowledge (memory) of particular social groups. This understanding of power takes account of the influence of social structure on knowledge.

There is a long list of authors who analyse power-knowledge. The study of power-knowledge derives from the perspective of sociology of knowledge, which studies the relationship between social context (particularly social structure) and forms of knowledge. This perspective can be found in the works of classical sociological theories: Marks, Mannheim, Weber or Stark. The concept of power-knowledge, however, is used in many disciplines: sociology, political sciences, international relations, philosophy, history, economics, urban studies, studies of education and science and many other fields.

Another problem relates to the definition of collective memory. It is one of the most problematic terms, which is demonstrated by the fact that there is a separate field of critical research on this concept (Olick 1999, 2007; Olick, Vinitzky-Seroussi and Levy 2011; Gedi and Elam 1996; Kansteiner 2002; Radstone 2000, 2008; Szacka 2006; Wertsch and Roediger 2008a, 2008b). As the definitions of power, knowledge and memory are unequivocal, there is a debate about what power-knowledge and power/memory actually refer to.

In my analysis, I will refer to several theories, authored by Eric Hobsbawm, John Bodnar, Michael Schudson, Richard Sennett and the so-called Popular Memory Group. I should start, however, with Michael Foucault, who coined the term power-knowledge – it appears in his work *The History of Sexuality* (1978: 98).[3] Foucault analyses the problem of power over collective memory in the field of mass culture and studies the transformations in collective memory in the context of broader transformations in mass society (Foucault 1975). He examined the mechanisms of power and knowledge, such as the role of authority or the category of truth. He also observed that relations of power-knowledge are dynamic and susceptible to change.[4]

Adopting a sociological perspective, Eric Hobsbawm analysed social mechanisms that regulate the process of forming collective memory. His concept of invented tradition explains the phenomenon of normative power over memory. According to Hobsbawm, constructing and instituting traditions is a form of power. The author demonstrated how power is exercised with the use of rituals. He also analysed the role of social order, noting that social change creates the need to invent traditions as a form of exercising power (Hobsbawm 2013). Richard Sennett, who also analysed the macrostructural context of power-knowledge, analysed the influence of the market on mentality and collective memory. In his opinion, conditions generated by late capitalism (such as impermanence, instability, lack of continuity or individualisation of labour) led to privatisation of memories and, as a result, to the vanishing of collective memory. Sennett (2006) observed that these factors caused a general crisis in the liberal culture of contemporary capitalism. Bodnar (1992), on the other hand, noted that collective memory reveals the structures of power in a society. As power is always questioned, collective memory becomes an instrument of power. Schudson (1989) presented an interesting theory of three factors that limit the full freedom to reconstruct the past: "the structure of available pasts, the structure of individual choices, and the conflicts about the past among a multitude of mutually aware individuals

---

3   Although he was the author of the term, he was not the first to analyse the relationship between power and knowledge. Similar concepts appeared in the works of many philosophers. The phrase *ipsa scientia potestas est* is commonly attributed to Francis Bacon (*Meditationes Sacrae*) and Hobbes in his *Leviathan* included an almost identical phrase *scientia potentia est*. While Bacon in his words referred to the power and knowledge of God, Hobbes referred to human abilities and the characteristics of their knowledge.

4   "Relations of power-knowledge are not static forms of distribution, they are matrices of transformations" (Foucault 1978: 99).

or groups" (107). Oral history studies provide another interesting perspective in the analysis of power-knowledge, as they take into consideration the influence of memories of common people on the shape of collective memory. In oral communication, history becomes a part of people's life experiences. The official, historical narrative is reinterpreted from individual and subjective perspectives, which demonstrates that collective memory is constituted from different forms of memory in an interactive process (Schudson 1993, 1989).

Power-knowledge as local politics of memory

Referring to the aforementioned theories, I am going to demonstrate that power over knowledge/memory is structurally limited. More precisely, it is limited by the structure of the socio-political situation and by culture: i.e., the stability of norms and values. This means that culture and structure are a context of forming the memory of the past.

A classic example of power-knowledge is the politics of memory:[5] attempts to influence collective memory with the (usually legal) power to create an official version of history using different methods (mass media, the education system, science, art, etc.), for example. The politics of memory is an instrument of control of the past as well as the present. For instance, it is used to gain power (as an element of a political campaign) and it is an instrument of power (legitimation and retaining power).

Many politicians attempt to use the past as an instrument of power with varied success, as power-knowledge has limitations – reconstruction of the past is limited by numerous factors. Schudson (1989), in his analysis of the factors that limit the freedom to reconstruct the past, focused on the structure of available pasts. The structure of available pasts consists of past experiences and events that constituted a tradition. What is more, some elements of this tradition "have emerged as particularly salient" (Ibid.) as a result of the so-called "rhetorical structure of social organisation that gives prominence to some facets of the past and not others" (Ibid.). Different types of media (museums, statues) are part of this process, as well as literary canons, anniversaries or public debates that make up the rhetorical power of facts in collective memory. The past events that have become elements of the public discourse gain rhetorical power and – as Schudson claims – they will

---

5   Polish literature on the subject is dominated by a historical and political perspective; see also Kosiewski and Cichocki (2008), Cichocki (2005), Nowinowski, Pomorski and Stobiecki (2008), Muller (2004). Muller believes that the relation between memory and power is a neglected area of research.

always remain, in one form or another, in collective memory (e.g. statues that have been built or rituals that have been established are difficult to remove). Even rare events can have enormous influence on collective memory – *originating events*, and traumatic events and catastrophes also cannot be removed from memory.

Wrocław myths

Power over memory (integrated into structural limitations) takes diverse forms. Symbolic social practices – rituals, commemorative events and official celebrations – are interesting examples. Eric Hobsbawm (2013) provides an analysis of the process of mythologisation of tradition and rituals as an important instrument of power. Referring to a fictional past, an invented tradition creates history for the purposes of the present. In other words, invented traditions are determined by current interests. The likelihood of this phenomenon increases in times of rapid social change. Such was the case of Wrocław in the post-war period of Polonisation and de-Germanisation, when the politics of memory created myths and rituals to support and legitimise this process (Thum 2008).

According to Hobsbawm, inventing traditions are governed by a set of rules of a ritual or symbolic nature that seek to inculcate certain values and norms of behaviour. Their repetition automatically implies continuity with the past, or, Hobsbawm adds, "in fact, where possible, they normally attempt to establish continuity with a suitable historical past" (Hobsbawm and Ranger 2013: 1). As the author notes, this continuity is "largely factitious". Hobsbawm distinguishes three (overlapping) types of invented traditions that are characteristics of industrial society: "a) those establishing or symbolising social cohesion or the membership of groups (…), b) those establishing or legitimising institutions, status or relations of authority, and c) those whose main purpose was socialisation, the inculcation of beliefs, value systems and conventions of behaviour". The first type is prevalent, "the other functions being regarded as implicit in or flowing from a sense of identification with a community and/or the institutions representing it, such as a nation". The reason why traditions are invented is the need to create cohesion in larger social entities that were not *Gemeinschaften* as a result of social mobility and class conflicts.

The so-called Wrocław myths[6] are examples of Hobsbawm's (b) type of invented tradition that establishes and legitimises the institutions of authority. Traces of this policy can still be seen in Wrocław. Politics of memory was and still is a form

---

6   Due to its ambiguity, myth is a controversial term. In this chapter I define myth as an untrue belief. For more on the use of myth in collective memory, see Pabjan (2016).

of power over the memory of the people of Wrocław. The authorities produce myths for the purpose of particular interests, e.g. the communist rulers invented the legitimisation myth of the Piast dynasty as first rulers of the city (the myth of the *Piast Land*).[7] The settlement of Polish people in Wrocław and repossession of the city's German heritage was defined as a *return to the roots*. This way, due to the myth (and the language that expressed it), negative phenomena (*taking over what is foreign*) were transformed into positive ones (*returning, regaining*). The narrative about history in academic and, particularly, popular literature followed the process of mythologisation, which helped to create convenient circumstances for the Polish settlement in Wrocław. The myths were meant to reduce the sense of strangeness and fear and to legitimise Polish power over the territories taken over from the Germans. Without these instruments of power it would have been much more difficult to encourage people to settle there and regain authority in the area. Myths were an element of the strategy to legitimise the new national borders (Thum 2008: 257–327).

Collective knowledge displays strong myth-creation tendencies: people are much more likely to believe in myths than to be interested in a detailed reconstruction of history (Sennett 2011: 284). The myths that were created in the times of the Polish People's Republic still function in collective memory. Table 1 demonstrates that the *Lvov myth* (the opinion that the majority of settlers came to Wrocław from Lvov) is still alive. 49% of the respondents believe that the settlers came from Lvov and 48% that they came from the east, including Lvov (97% altogether) but the belief that most of the Wrocław settlers came from the east is not true. The data from the 1950 census demonstrates that the settlers came from different places and only 30% of them from the eastern territories, including Lvov (Kosiński 1960).

Table 1: The Lvov myth

Former place of residence of the settlers according to the interviewees:	N=545 %
from Lvov	49
from the east	48
other or lack of regional identification	3

Source: *The Memory of Vanished populations, own research*

---

7   The question of whether the Piast were Poles is debatable.

As the study demonstrates, belief in myths is associated with one's education level. Higher cultural capital decreases the likelihood of being influenced by myths, and, consequently, of being influenced by the politics of memory that uses myths to reconstruct history. While half the population of Wrocław believes in the Lvov myth (see Table 1), students (16%) and the elite (10%) are less likely to share this belief (see Table 2).

Table 2: Belief in the Lvov myth

The Lvov myth: the belief that Wrocław settlers came from Lvov	WROCŁAW RESIDENTS		THE ELITE		STUDENTS	
	Frequency	%	Frequency	%	Frequency	%
Most Wrocław settlers came from Lvov	270	49.5	6	9.5	51	15.5
People from Lvov were the Wrocław cultural and intellectual elite	156	28.6	53	84.1	107	32.5
Many institutions from pre-war Lvov moved to Wrocław	43	7.9	4	6.3	49	14.9
I don't know	76	13.9	0	0	122	37.1
Overall	545	100.0	59	100.0	329	100.0

Source: *The Memory of Vanished populations*, own research

Today the local authorities also create myths to pursue their political and economic interests. For instance, the image of multicultural Wrocław is an element of the current development strategy oriented at foreign tourists (Kłopot 2012), which was materialised in the form of the District of Four Temples (known also as the District of Mutual Respect or the Quarter of Four Denominations).[8]

According to Hobsbawm's theory, by creating the myth, the local authorities in Wrocław participated in the process of creating tradition – they built historical continuity that united the old times with the new. Myths also have another role: they bond citizens together and strengthen their local identity. Due to the almost complete population exchange in post-war Wrocław, the continuity, tradition and identity with the place was broken. Myths that were aimed at building this identity were also in the interest of the authorities as they strengthened social integration. As Thum (2008: 215) aptly noted, "Speaking of the 'Recovered Territories' or the

---

8   I will return to this subject in other sections of this chapter.

return to 'Piast Land' was healing, a kind of therapy against the syndrome of impermanence". These two examples of myth, however, significantly differ. The myth of the Piast Land was created by politicians, while the Lvov myth was created by intellectuals. The former, therefore, refers to the second kind of tradition in Hobsbawm's theory – the tradition that legitimises power – while the latter myth represents the first kind of tradition – the tradition that expresses collective identity and builds social cohesion.

Photograph 1: The statue of Bolesław Chrobry

Source: Author's archive.

Rather than being isolated from national memory, local memory is usually incorporated into it (Bodnar 1992). In the case of Wrocław, local memory is rooted in a nationalist tradition, as the symbolic Polish-German conflict transfers the local problem onto a national level. This phenomenon is manifested in one of the examples of invented tradition: the annual march organised by nationalist groups in Wrocław on 11th November, Independence Day in Poland. The ritualised activities of nationalists centre on the memorial of Bolesław I the Brave, the first King of Poland. Far-right groups have taken over this memorial to use it as a symbol of the mythologised history of *Great Poland*. This phenomenon is an example of the first type of tradition distinguished by Hobsbawm (2013), which serves to increase social cohesion within far-right groups. If nationalist groups gained power, this tradition could transform into the second type. It is not clear whether the discussed monument significantly revived the collective memory. First of all, there are controversies over its meaning and symbolism. While the initiators of the project refer to the idea of a united Europe, nationalist groups refer to the idea of a strong Poland.

While grassroots traditions often become an important part of collective memory, arbitrarily invented traditions are socially dead. The latter only demonstrate the elite's interests, and the elite and society in general have conflicting interests, resulting from their different positions in the social structures that determine these interests. A much more effective strategy by the authorities to influence collective memory is to use myths. Both the Lvov myth and the Piast Land myth left permanent and false information about the city's history in the collective memory. Myths are effective because they are stories that address fundamental, existential questions (they explain who we are and where we are from). It should be again stressed that mythologisation is a cognitive process, which may be interpreted in anthropological terms: it serves to mark a group's territory and protect it. The authorities only use myths as an instrument – and they use them quite effectively, but only when they properly adopt the structure of myths and respond to social needs.

The District of Four Temples

Another example of the politics of memory and inventing local traditions is the so-called District of Four Temples project. It is an illustration of Eric Hobsbawm's (2013) theory of invented tradition, Terence Ranger's (2013) concept of the construction of identity and Michael Schudson's (1989) analysis of restrictions of freedom to reconstruct the past. Historical temples (architecture, history, religion) were used to create an *imagined place* that symbolises the idea of Wrocław as a multicultural, tolerant city that is open to other cultures – "the meeting place" (the official motto). The district also follows the discourse of the city's identity that was created by the elite. As the research results demonstrate, the activities undertaken by the political and intellectual elite are effective because the "multicultural Wrocław" slogan found its way into the collective conscious-ness and became an element of the popular image of the city. The study also demonstrated that most Wrocław citizens believe that their city was multicultural in the past and it still is. Only 10% of the respondents believed that Wrocław was not multicultural (see Fig. 1). However, statistical data proves the opposite: Wrocław was not multicultural in either the 19th or 20th century. National mi-norities (including the Polish and the Jewish minority) never exceeded 5% of the population. Although these estimations may not be precise, as at the time ethnicity was measured according to declared language and religion, the num-ber of culturally diverse populations of Wrocław was low (Knie J.G., 1830, *Die Gemeinden und Gutsbezirke des Preußischen Staates und ihre Bevölkerung 1874, Gemeindelexikon für die Provinz Schlesien. 1887, 1898, 1908, Statistische Daten über die Stadt Breslau 1901–1913*). Moreover, the residents quickly germanised to increase their chances of social promotion, which would have been otherwise impossible (Davis and Moorhouse 2011: 331–338). In other words, Wrocław was German before the war and it has been Polish since the war. Thus, the multicul-turalism of Wrocław is a myth.

Figure 1: The myth of multicultural Wrocław in collective memory

Is Wroclaw multicultural?

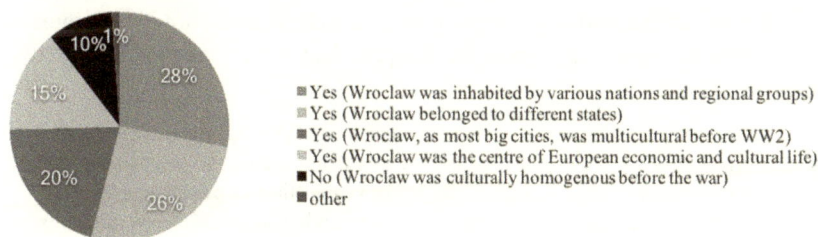

- Yes (Wroclaw was inhabited by various nations and regional groups)
- Yes (Wroclaw belonged to different states)
- Yes (Wroclaw, as most big cities, was multicultural before WW2)
- Yes (Wroclaw was the centre of European economic and cultural life)
- No (Wroclaw was culturally homogenous before the war)
- other

Source: *The Memory of Vanished populations*, own research

Does this example actually illustrate the effectiveness of the politics of memory, i.e. the power over memory? The popularity of slogans such as "Multicultural Wrocław", "Wrocław – the Meeting Place", "Wrocław – the Open City" in col-lective consciousness results mostly from their constant use. In many contexts and occasions – events, debates, advertisements etc. – the authorities use these slogans in their communication with the public. Frequent repetition leads to memorisation. However, in Hobsbawm's terms, does it result in the third type of tradition, the main purpose of which is socialisation? Popularity of an image does not necessarily mean its acceptance or internalisation. The question is whether there are any other indications that may demonstrate that Wrocław is perceived as a multicultural city. The gathered data suggests that on the contrary, Wrocław's multiculturalism is only a stereotype, a cliché, which is demonstrated by a study of the actual tolerance and openness of Wrocław residents. The study shows that the attitude of Wrocław residents to the German past of the city is complicated and rarely positive, particularly among the elite.[9]

The common reception of the District of Four Temples also proves that the elites failed to influence the collective memory by only developing this area and making it a symbol of the city's multiculturalism. While the idea of the district, which was initiated by religious communities, was to propagate interreligious dialogue and ecumenism, to support actions aimed at respecting history, tradition and culture and to encourage citizens to "love thy neighbour", the narratives about the district are ambivalent. The study results demonstrate that the residents mostly associate the district with entertainment, as cafes, bars and clubs are located in the vicinity of the religious and cultural institutions. While the intellectual elites (representatives of religious communities) stress religious and educational objectives behind the project (which correspond with Hobsbawm's third type of tradition), local authorities focus on the city's policy to market the district as a tourist attraction (Hobsbawm's second type of tradition). The ideological framework of the District of Four Temples project (based on tolerance and coexistence of different cultures and religions) is offered, as an in-demand product, to tourists from Western Europe. This is how the vice president of Wrocław presents the city's new historical politics:

> The District of Four Temples is an invaluable asset to the city's image and tourism. Anyone who visits Wrocław must come here and the inhabitants should also be encouraged to be here as often as in the Old Square – says Adam Grehl, the vice president of Wrocław. Renovation of heritage-listed buildings is important, but so are their new functions. People will visit this district not only because they want to see a pretty neighbourhood. They want to meet friends in a pub, sit in café terrace, have lunch or dinner, buy a book, visit an art gallery or atmospheric shops.[10]

---

9   This question will be discussed further in the chapter.
10 http://wroclaw.wyborcza.pl/wroclaw/1,36743,14113310,Awans_palacu_Ballestrem ow__Ma_byc_perla_dzielnicy.html#ixzz4G4qIHPIY: 1.08.2016.

The action programme related to the idea of cultural paths is aimed at the reconstruction of cultural values connected with this area and development of an attractive tourist path that will present the historical multiculturalism and contemporary openness of Wrocław.[11]

This example illustrates how the politics of memory becomes an element of the urban policy and, consequently, an element of the official, institutional memory created for the use of the city's tourism policy (Kłopot 2012). The politics of memory includes an ideological message; it refers to the ideas of tolerance, openness, multiculturalism, postmodernism and other popular slogan-keywords, which are addressed to educated people from the middle and upper-middle classes, particularly tourists from Western Europe, where multiculturalism is a demographical fact. However, the District of the Four Temples is not particularly popular among the general populace of Wrocław. The city residents do not know much about its location, origin or functions. Only 23% of the entire survey sample knew how the district originated while 63% of the elite knew it was an initiative of religious communities. Half of the respondents had no idea where the district is located and many of them gave vague directions, while among the elite the location was known. The results demonstrate that the district is not commonly recognised as a specific and distinguished area. As the District of the Four Temples is not an administrative unit, one might ask how it exists at all. It certainly is a kind of an *imagined space*. It is a symbolic space created by the elite and existing in their consciousness – but not in the collective consciousness. Referring again to Hobsbawm's theory, this place is not related to the tradition of the first type, which is aimed at creating social bonds and integrating the community through rituals. It integrates only a part of the elite, intellectuals and tourists rather than the inhabitants in general. No rituals have been constituted that the majority of the local community would share. The march that is organised every year at the anniversary of Kristallnacht gathers a tiny fraction of the local community. To conclude, the District of the Four Temples was created by intellectual and religious elites as an element of the politics of memory but the political elite took it over and used it as a political marketing tool, while the residents perceive this space as a centre of entertainment.

The limited power of the political and intellectual elite over collective memory results from the fact that collective consciousness is shaped by a certain system of values and beliefs, and the effectiveness of power-knowledge is high only when convergent with it. The project of the district does not refer to any collective

---

11 www.wrocław.pl.

experience or tradition of the local community. The idea of religious tolerance is abstract in Wrocław, as it does not stem from tradition or the experience of its inhabitants: Wrocław is a city that lacks continuity of identity and the pre-war multiculturalism is a myth (Davis and Moorhouse 2011). The politics of memory that refer to strange and abstract experiences is ineffective because people cannot identify with it. The community of Wrocław is monocultural and religiously homogeneous, as is the rest of Poland. The multicultural city created alongside the district is an imagined space. Tolerance towards different religions is an ideal rather than a fact that describes real social patterns of behaviour.

In conclusion, the project of the District of the Four Temples is ineffective as an element of the politics of memory. The district is an emanation of an ideology that is characteristic of leftist, well-educated and wealthy groups. It is also an example of the struggle between particular groups of interest with different concepts of collective memory. This problem will be analysed in the next section of this chapter.

Power as asymmetry of collective memories

The asymmetry of social structure means that people with different positions in this structure have different abilities to influence the knowledge of others. Therefore, power-knowledge results from the asymmetry of structure. Various institutions, agents or centres of power may shape collective memory depending on the position they hold and the resources they possess. Referring to the asymmetry in the division of power, researchers of collective memory distinguish between official and unofficial memory, public and private, institutionalised and not institutionalised, dominant and counter-memories, etc. Unprivileged forms of memory of niche social groups can result in significant and influential forms of memory and the degree of their influence is an indicator of the power of the elite to impose memory on society. Structural differentiation in forms of memory manifest themselves in (1) the relation of domination between different forms of memory (the elite and ordinary people) and (2) specific narratives (e.g. politically correct or incorrect).

As John Bodnar aptly notes, practices of commemoration involve conflicts between different interests of groups with different positions in social structure. While the elite use these practices as an instrument of power and to maintain their position, ordinary citizens, guided by the interests of their social group or local community, treat those practices as a leisure activity. Political leaders use commemorative practices as tools that help them to increase control. On a cultural level, commemorative practices serve as symbols that unite the divergent interests of diverse social groups. Commemoration, as well as tradition in general, create an interpretative framework and unite communities. This mechanism is used by the authorities and official institutions to increase social unity and citizens' loyalty (Bodnar 1992). According to Bodnar, public memory emerges at the intersection of official and unofficial cultural content. Official memory results from the activity of political leaders in various institutions (educational, military, governmental, etc.). Political leaders are interested in maintaining social cohesion and institutional stability, particularly the institutions of power, and they wish to maintain power. Management of collective memory, i.e. creation of particular interpretations of the past, serves this aim (Bodnar 1992).

Forms of collective power express immanent contradictions rooted in society that result from the functioning of the social system. Different social groups have their own versions of the past. These differences in interpretations are an expression of various types of contradictions in society, e.g. local and national structures, ethnic and national cultures, men and women, young and old, professionals and clients, workers and managers, leaders and followers, soldiers and their commanders (Bodnar 1992: 14). Public memory serves as a mediator between these competing and often contradictory versions of reality (Ibid.). Public memory "is produced from political discussion that involves (…) fundamental issues about the entire existence of a society: its organisation, structures of power, and the very meaning of its past and its present" (Bodnar 1992: 14).

The memory of the elite and the popular memory

The asymmetry of collective memory, which has its source in social structure, means first of all that the memory of the elite and of the public is different and there is limited transmission of memory between the two groups. The substantial role of the elite in shaping collective memory is a myth.[12]

The study presented in this chapter confirms the differences between the memory of the public and the elite. Moreover, there are also significant differences within the elite: between the power elite and other groups: local activists, scientists, journalists, etc.[13] The study involved the following elements of collective memory: the knowledge of local history and attitudes towards it, oral history and intergenerational communication, commemorative practices that are important

---

12 However, there are cases when the influence of the elite is strong (as in the case of the settlement myths).

13 These differences are described in the first section of the chapter and illustrated by the case of the District of the Four Temples and Independence Day. Other examples will be discussed further in the text.

for reinforcing collective memory, the memory of German Wrocław (Breslau) in the collective consciousness and the level of tolerance to the commemoration of German heritage. The results demonstrate differences between the elite and other social groups in the declared frequency of commemorative practices. They are presented in Figure 2. It is clear that the average frequency level among the elite is higher for all types of activities. For the most popular practice across all groups, a tour around the city with friends, the average score among the elite is 1.95 while it is 1.4 for the general populace of Wrocław.[14] For other types of activities, the differences are even bigger. The average frequency of visiting history exhibitions was 1.92 for the elite, 0.94 for students and 0.82 for the Wrocław populace. Participation in commemorative events marking Wrocław historical anniversaries was 1.73 for the elite, 0.76 for the Wrocław populace and 0.68 for students.

Figure 2: Differences in commemorative practices between three groups (Wrocław populace, the elite and students)

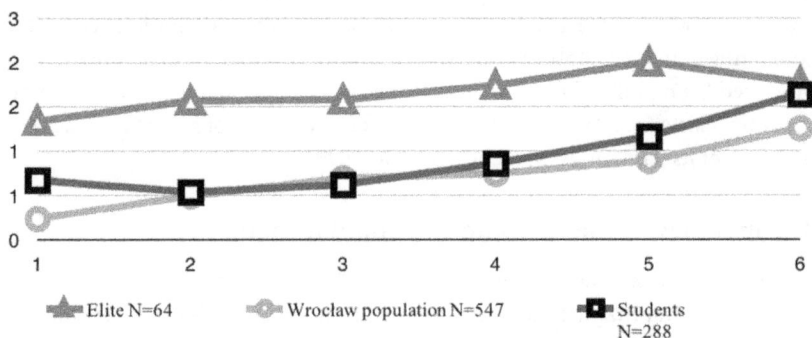

Elite N=64   Wrocław population N=547   Students N=288

1. Attending lectures on city history
2. Buying books about old Wrocław
3. Commemorating the history of Wrocław
4. Visiting exhibitions on the history of Wrocław
5. Reading books about history of Wrocław
6. Doing guided tours

Source: *The Memory of Vanished populations*, own research

Another form of activity – everyday conversations about Wrocław and the transmission of oral memory – is also most frequent among the elite. 67% of the elite declared that they often talked about Wrocław while only 25% of the general

---

14 Where 0 means never and 3 means very often.

Wrocław populace did so. As for the younger generation, 40% of students and 34% of pupils often talk about their city (see Figure 3).

Figure 3: Transmission of oral memory. Comparison between four samples: Wrocław populace, the elite, students and pupils.

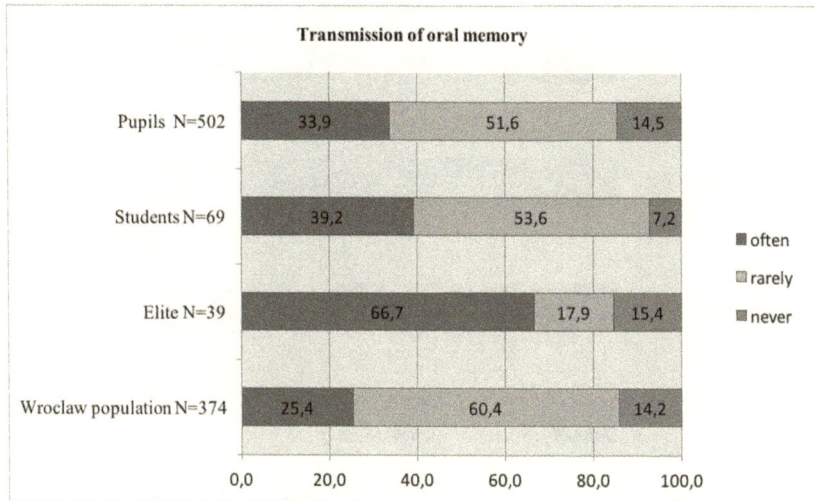

Source: *The Memory of Vanished populations,* own research

Another question studied in the research concerned the value attached to sites of memory. Do symbolic values of memorials dominate over utilitarian aspects? Respondents were asked whether memorials should be demolished when they come into conflict with the functional needs of the city. Members of the elite were less inclined to keep memorials and they declared more than twice as often as the general populace that "current city needs are more important and the need to keep memorials should be subordinate to those needs" (46% and 19%, see Figure 4).

Figure 4: *Comparison of attitudes to memorials among Wrocław citizens, students and the elite (data in percentages)*

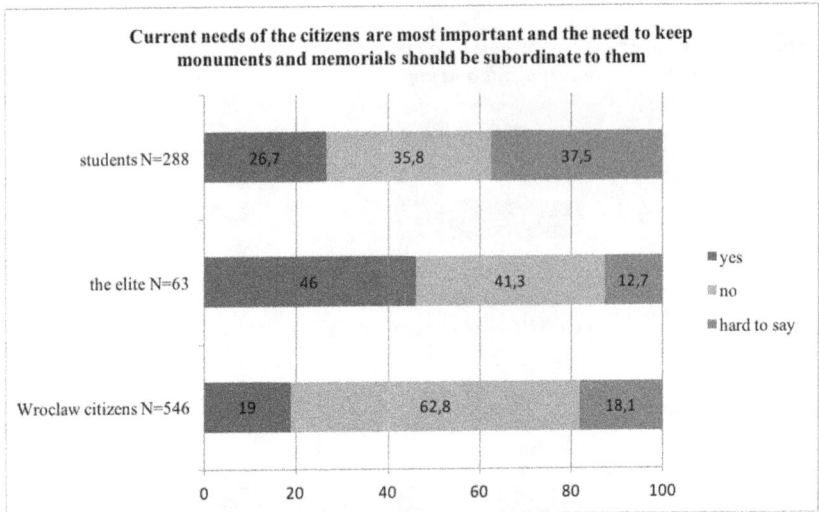

Current needs of the citizens are most important and the need to keep monuments and memorials should be subordinate to them

	yes	no	hard to say
students N=288	26,7	35,8	37,5
the elite N=63	46	41,3	12,7
Wroclaw citizens N=546	19	62,8	18,1

0   20   40   60   80   100

Source: *The Memory of Vanished populations,* own research

These differences may be explained by the fact that the elite, who manage the material substance of the city, are guided by pragmatic economic criteria (economic resources increase the range of power and monuments generate costs) and organisation of urban life. Citizens, on the other hand, who do not make decisions concerning the city, interpret the discussed dilemma in isolation from the problem of costs and they tend to focus on the symbolic aspect. Similarly, when asked about important criteria that should be considered when a decision about the renovation of historical buildings is being made, ordinary citizens and students pointed at the symbolic representation of Polish identity much more often than the elite. The elite, on the other hand, twice as often as other citizens, pointed out the symbolic representation of power as an important criterion. The difference in interests that influence the form of collective memory is also illustrated by the response to another question in the study. It refers to a building[15] constructed in the time and style of the monumental classicism of the Third Reich. The building is

---

15 The building, designed by Felix Bräuler in the style of the monumental classicism that was typical for the Third Reich, was dedicated to the new German authorities. The earliest blueprints come from 1935 and construction lasted from 1939 to 1945 (Dobesz 1998, 1999). 71% of the citizens do not know the origin and symbolism of the building.

a symbolic representation of Nazism as an element of the historical heritage of the city. The respondents were asked whether current use of this building by the local authorities as an administrative office (Voivodship Office) is appropriate or not. The difference between the elite and ordinary citizens is again considerable. The answer "definitely appropriate" was chosen by 90% of the elite, 55% of the Wrocław populace and 39% of students (Table 3). Most citizens and students did not know what the origin of the building was before they were asked the question (Table 4).

Table 3: *Symbolic and pragmatic values of the Voivodship Office, constructed in the Third Reich in 1939. Differences between the general Wrocław populace, students and the elite.*

Is it appropriate for the local authorities in Wrocław to use the Voivodship Office building, which was constructed and used by the Nazis?	The elite N=64	Wrocław citizens n=544	Students N=288
Absolutely appropriate	92.2	55.1	38.9
Somewhat appropriate	3.1	30.9	42.4
Yes and no	3.1	11.6	17.4
Somewhat inappropriate	1.6	1.5	1.4
Extremely inappropriate	0	0.9	0

Source: *The Memory of Vanished populations,* own research

Table 4: *Knowledge of the origin of the Voivodship Office in Wrocław*

Did you know that the building of the current Voivodship Office in Wrocław was constructed by the Nazis?	The elite N=64	Wrocław citizen N=547	Students N=288
Yes	85.9	28.9	34.7
No	14.1	71.1	65.3

Source: *The Memory of Vanished populations,* own research

The so-called ordinary citizens sometimes do not share the perspective of the authorities, expressing indifference to commemorative practices, or producing their own versions of memory. This phenomenon was also observed in the study:[16] there is a contradiction between official and elitist forms of memory and the memory of ordinary citizens (Bodnar 1992). Alternative forms of memory sometimes might become a cause of conflict. Strong differences between official and vernacular

---

16 This problem was also analysed earlier in this chapter, when discussing the District of the Four Temples and the memorial of Boeslaus I the Brave in the context of the differences in official and unofficial memory.

memory appear when these two types of memory refer to different values and experiences, particularly when witnesses of the historical events that are presented in official memory are still alive. Rosenzweig and Thelen (1998) note that individuals who experienced events that are presented in an official historical narrative perceive them from their personal, local perspective. This phenomenon may be observed also in reference to the collective memory of Wrocław citizens. The events that are elements of personal experiences are the main content of memory. Rather than events regarded by the political elite or historians to be elements of history, people mostly remember the most recent significant collective experiences. This tendency is confirmed by the research results. Wrocław citizens best remember the events that were recent, that affected the entire community and became a part of a collective experience. The most frequently listed events were the 1997 flood (48%) and the 2012 European Football Championship (31%). The collective memory of the events before 1945 is empty. Only 36 respondents mentioned the fact that Wrocław changed nationality and 13 people referred to the medieval origin of the people. Another difference between the elite and ordinary citizens was observed: 81% of the residents of Wrocław could not remember (did not know) any person or event in Wrocław history that would be worth commemoration, while there were hardly any respondents among the elite who gave such an answer (see Figure 5.1 and 5.2).

Figure 5.1 and 5.2: Differences in forms of collective memory (of pre-war Wrocław) between 3 groups of respondents

In your opinion, are there any events in Wroclaw history (up to1939) that should be commemorated?

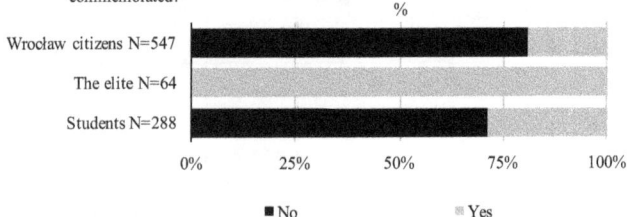

In your opinion, are there any historical figures from the most distant history of the city up to 1939 who should be particularly remembered in Wroclaw today?

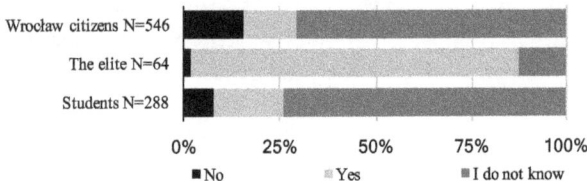

Source: *The Memory of Vanished populations,* own research

As a natural disaster, floods affect the entire community. It is a collective experience of a fundamental threat, thus the fact that it is remembered is not surprising. The other strongly remembered event is the 2012 European Football Championship, which was an important event taking place at the time of the research and an example of the influence of the media and the elite in defining the significance of events in the public space. This influence is usually apparent when one observes changing preferences and opinions depending on the current context of events. Contexts of events for different time periods create distinct forms of generational memory: each generation builds its own social biography consisting of significant collective events. Memory is generational knowledge, and collective experiences create an interpretative frame. The generational frame of interpreting history is an important context of the power-knowledge mechanism, which means that the power over collective memory is limited by generational experiences (see e.g. Schuman and Corning 2016; Cornig and Schuman 2015; Szacka 2006; Wertsch 2004; Igartua and Paez 1997; Schuman, Belli and Bischoping 1997; Conway 1997; Schuman and Scott 1989).

Intense politics of memory in the post-war era in the form of historical education was also analysed by Gregor Thum in his valuable work, quoted earlier (2008: 258–267). However, empirical studies of collective memory that focus on historical knowledge demonstrate the ineffectiveness or limitations of the politics of memory, particularly in the field of education (textbooks and curricula). A study of high school (final year) and university students in Wrocław, which was an element of the Memory of Vanished Populations research project, also demonstrated that they show a lack of local historical awareness or collective memory related to local history. The youth have little historical knowledge of the region and the city. They rarely attend commemorative events and they do not notice historical buildings or sites of memory, although the curriculum includes a so-called regional learning path.[17]

---

17 See e.g. http://dodn.wroclaw.pl/index.php/dolnoslaskie-sciezki; Regulation of the Minister of National Education of 27 August 2012 on the core curriculum and general education in certain types of schools, published in the Official Gazette on 30 August 2012, pos. 977. One of the authors studying the issue of regional teaching, Dzierżymir Jankowski, defines regional education as "introducing individuals and small groups to the tradition and current socio-cultural life of the region and the local environment". According to another author, Peter Petrykowski, the essential purpose of regional education is to "develop in young people the sense of regional self-identity as an attitude of commitment to the functioning of their environment and genuine openness to other communities and cultures".
http://dbp.wroc.pl/biblioteki/strzelin/images/Dokumenty/ut.pdf, accessed 1 July 2016.

Some of the intellectual elite respect the memory of German Wrocław and its German heritage. This attitude is not widely accepted, but evokes a diverse social response. Why is the idea of commemorating German past resisted? As already mentioned, this resistance results from the rhetorical structure of social organisation (using Schudson's terms). From the perspective of Wrocław residents, the commemoration of a nation that earlier inhabited their territory is against the interests of the local community, it questions the Polish identity of the city and causes a sense of territorial insecurity. World War II still casts a shadow on Polish-German relations. Perceiving themselves as victims, Poles believe that commemoration of German heritage contradicts their sense of justice. The power of the elite manifests itself in managing the structure of this situation, mainly by fuelling certain emotions. To exercise influence, political leaders need to refer to already existing frameworks of interpretation, such as those based on fears and conflicts. Therefore, references to German resentment and rejection of German heritage provide fertile ground for the authorities while affirmative attitudes need considerable effort to be adopted.

The politics of memory is related to the sphere of values, which manifests itself in how particular social groups attach different importance to history and share their specific visions of history (e.g. models of history are created around values such as nation or homeland). How are attitudes to the commemoration of the past different? Respondents were asked to agree or disagree with several statements, which were indicators of different models of the politics of memory. For instance, 36% of Wrocław citizens, 63% of students and 92% of the elite agreed with the statement *Commemoration of former residents and the multicultural character of Wrocław is in fact a hidden attempt to Germanise Wrocław citizens*. A similar tendency was observed in responses to another statement. 35% of Wrocław citizens, 42% of students and 78% of the elite agreed with the statement: *Commemoration of old residents and the multicultural character of Wrocław provides new arguments for the German federations of expellees*. Finally, 36% of Wrocław citizens, 45% of students and 83% of the elite (more than double the percentage of ordinary citizens) agreed with the statement: *The restoration of pre-war names of streets and objects is a symbolic Germanisation of Wrocław*. The results demonstrate considerable differences between the elite, the students and the general populace. They also show that the elite more often share the model of history that involves defence of Polish identity of the city. Compared to Wrocław citizens, the elite are less in favour of the idea of commemoration, particularly the commemoration of German heritage. Aside from far-right and nationalist politicians, this standpoint is not officially presented, which means that the real opinions of the political leaders may be suppressed by political correctness.

The reluctance of the elite to acknowledge the Jewish heritage of the city is equally strong. 40% of Wrocław citizens, 62% of students and 92% of the elite agreed with the statement: *The restoration of pre-war names of streets and objects is a symbolic appropriation of the city by the Jews*. Responses to another statement (*Commemoration of old residents and the multicultural character of Wrocław is in fact a hidden attempt by the Jews to regain their lost material goods*) confirmed this attitude: 48% of Wrocław citizens, 63% of students and 94% of the elite agreed with the statement. The elite were also more radical in their opinions, choosing the answer "strongly agree" more frequently than other respondents.

While there may be a problem of drawing general conclusions about the attitudes of the Wrocław political and cultural elite[18] from this non-representative sample (N=64), it is interesting to observe that similar attitudes (commemoration as a material and symbolic threat) were adopted among respondents with a university education from the general populace sample. This phenomenon is surprising, considering that tolerance and openness usually increase with education. It can be explained by the fact that the commemoration of Germans or Jews is perceived as contrary to the interests of the elite: as an unpopular attitude, it may be widely criticised and used as a tool in political struggle (promoting the commemoration of German heritage is perceived as contrary to Polish interests). Another explanation is that political and cultural leaders have a better knowledge of history and thus they are more influenced by popular models of historical education and oral memory, in which German resentment is strong (see Fronczyk and Łada 2009; Łada 2010, 2011; Osiński 2010; Pawełczyńska 1975; Szacka 2006; Thum 2008; CBOS 2006, 2014). The obtained results support a second interpretation, because education level is the largest differentiating factor for commemoration of German heritage.

Another characteristic phenomenon I would like to analyse is the discrepancy between the official and unofficial memory of the elite. Political correctness and tolerance, officially presented, are only a façade. The difference between the public discourse, which represents a declarative model of the politics of memory (the elite say what they are expected to say) and the real interests of the elite – is very important for the analysis of actual power over memory. An analogical phenomenon was described by Gregor Thum in reference to the communist politics of memory. While the communist authorities used the term "de-Germanisation, eliminating

---

18 The elites studied included city officials, councillors, academics, architects, politicians and journalists. Generally, two groups dominated: high-ranking city officials and intellectuals.

the vestiges of Germandom" in confidential documents, the officially employed term was "re-Polonisation" (Thum 2008: 214–215).

Cognitive models of memory

Forms of memory that are alternative to the official memory demonstrate that the elite's power over popular memory is limited. The study presented in this chapter confirms this phenomenon: there are significant discrepancies between the memory of the elite and Wrocław residents. A cluster analysis was conducted that included statements representing axiological orientation towards commemoration policy. The average response to particular statements was also analysed. Data analysis confirmed the existence of different patterns of memory, which I propose to present as two cognitive models of memory, i.e. the symbolic model and the discursive model. The former measured the attitude to different forms of commemoration in the symbolic space and the latter measured the attitude to certain narratives characteristic to the debate about commemoration of German heritage, particularly involving the Regained Territories. While the symbolic model of memory focused on significant places (specific buildings and objects in Wrocław), the discursive model involved general statements about the identity of places, place attachment and the role of the authorities in the process of commemoration. The characteristics of models are presented in Table 5.

Table 5: Characteristics of symbolic and discursive models.

symbolic model	discursive model
place	concept
visual representation	abstract
concrete exemplification	universal rules
territorial	intellectual concepts
remembrance of place	norms of remembrance
memory media	interpretations of the historical facts

Research results demonstrate that Wrocław citizens and the elite differ with respect to the two models of memory. The general populace is against forms of commemoration that involve changes to the urban space and, more often than the elite, they declare a positive attitude towards commemoration in general (the discursive model). The elite, on the contrary, are more likely to accept commemoration in the urban space than in the sphere of discourse.[19] The symbolic model scale referred to actual changes in the urban space and measured attitudes to different forms of commemoration (reconstruction/restoration of buildings and memorials, changes of names, returning ownership of buildings to religious-cultural communities) of different buildings/objects (memorials, temples, a shop, a theatre, a bridge) with different ethnic/cultural identities (Polish, German, Jewish). Both models included the attitude to ethnic groups (the Jews and the Germans). The interviewees were presented with statements that proposed changes in the urban space and they were asked to declare how much they agree or disagree with these proposals. As for the discursive scale, the interviewees were given statements that described the normative model of the politics of memory. They included:

- Statements including the ethnic factor (Polish, Jewish and German)
- Statements including indicators of place attachment
- Statements expressing relations (potential conflict) between the identity of a space and commemoration of former residents of the city.

The comparison of responses to particular statements (see Tables 6 and 7) demonstrates that the elite and students have similar opinions concerning the ethnic factor, while they differed in terms of the identity factor (i.e. statements regarding place attachment). In the symbolic model, the commemoration of German heritage is less commonly accepted than the commemoration of Jewish heritage, mainly because the former would require more significant changes in the urban space. In the discursive model, the elite more frequently present an anti-Jewish than anti-German attitude, while the same correlation is weaker in the general populace (for more, see Tables 6 and 7). It is important to note that detailed analysis of the statements and the researched sample revealed more differentiation of memory patterns. For instance, the results demonstrate differences between particular professional groups among the elite. The attitude to commemoration is less positive in the case of officials than the liberal professions. In other words, those with more political power are more against the idea of commemoration. The results show that symbolic, discursive and ethnic aspects are most important when explaining memory differentiation. The cognitive and ethnic relationships models make it possible to systematically capture the differences between elite and popular memory (see Table 8).

---

19 The average level of acceptance for symbolic commemoration in the urban space was very low for the general populace (0.17, on a scale 0–1, where 1 was highest) and higher among the elite (0.33) and students (0.39). As for the discursive model, the average result was 0.43 for the general populace, 0.32 for students and only 0.14 for the elite.

How can we explain the differences in forms of memory and, consequently, the limited possibility of influence outside one's own social group? Memory, as social knowledge, is influenced by diverse social and cultural practices and social experience of reality that is also diverse (Rydgren 2007; DiMaggio 1997; Swidler 1986). The differing social situations of the elite and the residents create different cognitive contexts for memory: political and professional interests or cognitive structures influenced by higher education, professional independence or management positions. The social categories, symbols and language used by people to experience reality are different for different social groups (Swidler 1986). The politics of memory in urban space[20] is more important for the general public because it is more cognitively available. While the residents experience the consequences of the politics of memory in their urban space, they rarely participate in public debates about the shape of this politics. It refers to the well-known cognitive rule: people use the availability heuristic (Tversky and Kahenman 1973). The elite, on the other hand, focus on the intellectual discourse in which they participate and which is an element of their cultural capital. While the elite's structure of beliefs is developed and so are their concepts of memory (they have 'active memory'), the memory of the general populace is more latent ('passive memory'). People's beliefs are usually not fully articulated until they are provoked by some events or the debates of the elite (Bourdieu 2005). Similarly to the differences between the elite and the general populace, there are also differences of opinion within the latter group that are related to their education level. Education changes cognitive competences. Those whose knowledge of history is better are more aware of the significance of Polish-German conflicts and they take them into account when discussing contemporary politics of memory in Wrocław, where the commemoration of the Germans can hardly be neutral. On the contrary, those who are not interested in history are more indifferent[21] about the past. To conclude, the alternative models of memory demonstrate a lack of community between the elite and the general populace and call into question the elite's influence on social interpretations of the past.

---

20 By using city symbols to mark the identity of places, e.g. giving Polish names to streets, bridges and monuments.

21 The study demonstrated less interest in history among the general populace than among the elite.

Table 6: Accepted model of the politics of memory: comparison of two scales (mean values: min 0, max 1).

Acceptance of commemoration:	General populace of Wrocław	The elite	Students
discursive model	0.43	0.14	0.32
symbolic model	0.17	0.33	0.39

Source: *The Memory of Vanished populations*, own research.

Table 7: Comparison of average results on the acceptance scale (mean values: min 0, max 1) for ethnic relations (anti-German and anti-Jewish statements) and place attachment.

Comparison of average results on the acceptance scale for the general populace of Wrocław, the elite and the students			
Conflictual ethnic relations	Wrocław populace	The elite	Students
Anti-German (the symbolic model)	0.13	0.26	0.31
Anti-Jewish (the symbolic model)	0.28	0.46	0.54
Anti-Jewish (the discursive model)	0.45	0.22	0.35
Anti-German (the discursive model)	0.49	0.39	0.26
Place attachment (the discursive model)	0.38	0.15	0.32
The ethnic dimension: discursive model, all statements	0.48	0.32	0.33

Source: *The Memory of Vanished populations*, own research.

Table 8: Memory types, categorised by the cognitive model and the types of ethnic relationship.

MODELS:		cognitive	
		symbolic model	discursive model
TYPES OF ETHNIC REALTIONS	conflictual (anti-German)	popular memory	elite memory
	consensual (pro-German)	elite memory	popular memory

Source: *The Memory of Vanished Populations*, own research.

Institutional power over memory

Collective memory is to a large extent created by institutions, which initiate various activities that generate and materialise knowledge (e.g. publishing) and organise commemorative practices (e.g. commemorative cultural events). Local, urban institutions, including non-governmental organisations, often create alternative forms of collective memory. How do Wrocław institutions participate in creating collective memory? Do they contribute to creating the dominant version of memory or do they produce counter-memories?

As any other city, Wrocław has institutions that create narratives about the city and its past. For instance, the University Museum and city museums display exhibitions that present certain visions of the city's history. There are also various non-governmental organisations dedicated to the city's past and to other cultures and ethnic groups – which are major issues in the politics of memory in Wrocław. Citizen involvement in these organisations is negligible: only 1% of the general populace of Wrocław declare membership of a local history society. Therefore, the members may be classified as the elite.

Grassroots organisations that participate in creating commemorative narratives are e.g.: the Edith Stein Foundation, the Bente Kahan Foundation, the Society for Beautifying the City of Wrocław (Towarzystwo Upiększania Miasta), the Society of Friends of Wrocław (Towarzystwo Miłośników Wrocławia), the Foundation for the Mutual Respect of the Four Denominations (Fundacja Dzielnica Wzajemnego Szacunku Czterech Wyznań), the German Social and Cultural Society (Niemieckie Towarzystwo Społeczno-Kulturalne) and the Educational Society Babel Tower (Stowarzyszenie Edukacyjne Wieża Babel). There are also web portals dedicated to the history of Wrocław, which display photographs, information, films, and maps, and analyse the differences between pre-war and contemporary Wrocław, including street names. Moreover, the Via Nova Publishers publish works devoted to the city's history and German heritage in Wrocław.[22]

Even a cursory analysis of the activity of Wrocław institutions demonstrates that they create alternative forms of memory, which in some aspects differ from popular and official memory. The grassroots movements promote a normative model of memory that involves tolerance and acceptance of the multicultural tradition of Wrocław and direct references to the German history of the city. This model manifests itself in the programmes of many institutions and it is a manifestation of the assumed role of the elite to set behaviour patterns. Political elites interpret the German history of Wrocław differently. This subject is treated as sensitive and references to it are usually very cautious.

---

22 I only briefly present the activities of non-governmental institutions in Wrocław. An in-depth description is beyond the scope of this chapter. For more, see e.g. the website of the Society of Friends of Wrocław (Towarzystwo Miłośników Wrocławia), which presents the diverse educational activities of this organisation. (http://tmw.com.pl/)

The media are another source of influence on collective memory. In this chapter I will analyse selected examples of media participation in the local discourse on collective memory. The fundamental question in this context concerns the extent of the media's influence on collective memory. I share the opinion that the media cannot influence the content of normative beliefs, i.e. the axiological orientation of the collective memory. The media act as a communication platform and an actor who represents the elites. Their power is potential and it mostly means the power to deliver information to a wide audience and manage the public debate by selecting subjects and intensifying emotional messages. In this case, power-knowledge lies in access to specific technical means and means of emotional persuasion. The other fundamental question that needs to be answered is to whom the media belong and whose memory they promote.[23] Put briefly, the media belong to the elite. Any limitation of the elite's power in the media is a result of the changing forms of communication thanks to the internet. The opportunities to create, provide, exchange and receive information have increased due to technological changes. Thanks to the internet, "ordinary people" not only have easier and cheaper access to information, they also became active recipients and senders of information and they can be involved to a greater degree in the public debate. The internet brought about changes in the scope of power.

A debate on a series of articles in *Gazeta Wyborcza* (one of the leading Polish newspapers) serves as an empirical illustration of the power of the media. The articles by Beata Maciejewska were dedicated to the history of German Wrocław. The author attempted to popularise knowledge of the German heritage of the city and to promote the idea of tolerance and acceptance of the city's German past. Her articles started an internet debate among the readers, which revealed differences in the forms of collective memory. Here are several examples of the points raised in the debate.

> For three days in a row there have been articles in *Gazeta Wyborcza* about how we need to commemorate Germans, each is more aggressive than the last, some groups seem to know how to get things their own way – unlike our dear nation… [wesoly_emigrant].[24]

---

23 Media influence is the subject of a separate and broad field of studies. Here, I only intend to signalise the problems related to media influence that is important for the presented research results.

24 All the quotations in this section are from *Gazeta Wyborcza*, 12 and 14 February 2011. The usernames of the commenters are provided in brackets.

This stranger is not my hero, he's certainly a hero for the Germans, not for me, though. For me he's a guy who did great things and that's it, I'm not going to consider him my hero. [wesoly_emigrant]

If someone is reluctant to cherish Prussian traditions in Wrocław (the Royal Palace, the Centennial Hall) and if he or she only asks whether it makes sense to honour an enemy of Poles in a Polish city, they are accused of inciting hatred against nationality and returning to 1939. Your rhetoric is similar to Maciejewska's [the author of the article] but you went even further. And if someone is inciting hatred here (ok, let's not exaggerate – if someone is causing conflicts and waking national phobias) it is actually Maciejewska. [pingwiniarz]

I'm fed up with her [the author's] modern (…) historically accurate European views and the accompanying insinuation that whoever disagrees with her is an obscurantist. What I protest against is thoughtless glorification of the past of this city, which we as Poles have reasons not to cherish. And what makes me boil with rage is Maciejewska and her rhetoric, that is, whoever is against the Royal Palace is a dunce who's afraid of Germans returning to their *Heimat*. [pingwiniarz]

The subject [of the article] is the commemoration of the outstanding mayor of Breslau who "by the way" (as someone pointed out) wrote a very nationalistic book. I believe that one should always remember, particularly here in Wrocław, about the tragic consequences of implementing nationalism into the political doctrine. If Georg Bender deserves to be remembered positively as a mayor and negatively as a German nationalist, I would support the idea of putting up a commemorative plaque in this park and provide both pieces of information: one glorifying and one cautionary. This would be a clear signal that proves our respect for the past. However, we should carefully avoid commemorating ANY events, institutions or people from the Nazi period of Breslau. In this context, celebrating the 100th anniversary of technical universities in Wrocław was a major political mistake that the University Senate or rectors unfortunately did not understand. [WK]

The debaters seem to use the article as an opportunity to reveal their opinions rather than think about them or modify them. As a result, the representative of the elite, Beata Maciejewska (a historian), has little chance to persuade the readers who think differently to share her opinion. The major effect of the article, which is observable in the internet debate, is the polarisation of opinions.

Some readers interpret Maciejewska's article as promotion of pro-German cultural politics (which several comments clearly suggest). As Foucault noted, the struggle over history is focused on how to re-programme popular memory and impose interpretative frames on people. "People are shown not what they were but what they must remember having been" (Foucault 2011: 253). However, in the case of collective memory in Wrocław, the persuasive power of the intellectual elite does not seem effective, despite numerous attempts to refer to the city's German heritage in a positive way. Empirical arguments support this theory: the quoted comments and the data related to the debate about Bender or Independence Day suggest that the reluctance to consider the commemoration of the German past of Wrocław is not decreasing despite the elite's efforts.

In conclusion, the collective memory of contemporary Wrocław residents includes a discursive and symbolic model, **both of which include two types: a conflictual and consensual.** The consensual type involves an attempt to peacefully come to terms with the past, end the Polish-German conflict and commemorate the German past of Wrocław. The conflictual type involves anti-German attitudes and continues to use World War II as a framework of interpretation for contemporary events. On the basis of the Memory of Vanished Populations study, which is repeatedly quoted in this chapter, one may conclude that the discursive model of conflictual Polish-German relations dominates in the collective memory of the elite, while the symbolic model of conflictual ethnic relations dominates in the collective memory of Wrocław residents[25] (see Table 8). The structure of historical events and their specific character (the WW2 trauma) determine the interpretative framework for the past (Schudson 1989). As the Polish-German war was a national conflict, global interpretation dominates over the local one. It is difficult to determine precisely how popular this way of perceiving history is because particular opinions differ, as does the emotional intensity that accompanies them. In other words, rather than one homogeneous anti-German attitude, internally differentiated and complex attitudes were revealed in the studied population.[26] On the basis of the results it may be estimated that anti-German resentments apply to around one-quarter to one-third of the study population but their intensity differs and it depends on the definition of the conflict and the measurement method. Nationwide surveys confirm that the burden of World War II is still present in the Polish collective consciousness. Asked whether World War II continues to burden contemporary relations, 34% of Poles agreed in 2005, 43% in 2008 and 39% in 2009 (ISP 2005, 2008, 2009). In another survey, 20% of respondents believed that the events of World War II remain a burden, 42% believed that they influence Poles' attitude to Germans. 16% also expressed a feeling of threat related to territorial claims, and 49% of respondents felt that such claims were likely (Instytut Demoskopii w Allensbach 2011; Łada 2010, 2011).[27]

Michel Foucault's perspective and his focus on the dynamic character of social knowledge is very useful in the analysis of the research results. Polish collective

---

25 Conversely, the symbolic consensual model is characteristic of the memory of the elites, and the discursive consensual model for popular memory.

26 A scale was developed to measure anti-German attitude: a series of statements with which the respondents agreed or disagreed to varying degrees.

27 See Fałkowski (2006, 2011), Fałkowski and Popko (2006a, 2006b, 2006c).

memory includes a potentially negative interpretative framework for Polish-German relations, which was developed as a result of the politics of memory. Power-knowledge today involves managing this framework, either by accentuating it or reducing the level of conflict – usually the former (e.g. fuelling negative emotions in political campaigns).

The variability of forms of knowledge results from the dynamics of the power-knowledge relations in the context of local politics and the functioning of local democracy and media discourse. A study of the collective memory of a local community should also involve an examination of the memory mechanism from a macrosocial perspective. Power over collective memory in Wrocław results from social conditions that stimulate the emergence of institutions, patterns of behaviour or systems of beliefs, etc. From this perspective, as well as from a Marxist perspective, power-knowledge involves shaping the forms and content of beliefs in particular social conditions. Thus, forms of memory may and should be explained as a result of the influence of particular social conditions. Wrocław's collective memory is embroiled in the political and economic processes that the city has been going through: Poland's membership of the EU and opening to the global market of economy and culture. Wrocław has become a site of investments made by international corporations. Economic and political changes became a foundation of the visions of the future and the past created by the elite. International contacts are much more often established among the cultural and business elite than ordinary citizens, which means that the elite's attitude to other cultures and nations may be more positive. In other words, political and economic interests are a structural groundwork that foster the development of positive attitudes to other cultures, which probably results from the identification of some intellectuals with pro-European values. But only some members of the elite share this attitude. The official politics of memory also follow this standing, which is an element of a governance strategy. Wrocław is promoted as a multicultural city, a welcoming meeting place. Although this project refers to the ideological sphere, the underlying causes are in fact economic. The multicultural slogan is a strategy to attract investors and to make tourism one of the fundamental sources of the city's income.

Collective memory is also influenced by the capitalist system, as Sennett (2006) observes. Capitalism stimulates the growth of social individualism or even isolationism, which results from the form of organisation of labour (individualisation of labour), workplace mobility, as well as the orientation towards change and the future rather than the past. This form of capitalism shapes new cultural patterns – a new perception of time (Ibid.).[28] This influence applies also to knowledge, including collective memory. Sennett believes that the capitalist economy leads to individualisation and privatisation of memories, which results in disintegration of collective memory. Memory becomes increasingly subjective, private and de-institutionalised. A community of memory cannot develop in an individualised society. It appears as a result of interactions and through them, even if it is diverse. Thus, capitalist economy impedes the development of collective memory.

To conclude, local collective memory is shaped in the context of cultural and macrostructural transformations.

Conclusions

Based on empirical data, the author demonstrated that the elite's power over collective memory has its limitations. The elite's power mainly manifests itself in the domination of public discourse, as the authorities control access to memory media. However, their persuasive power, or the opportunity to impose forms of memory, is limited. This manifests itself in the discrepancy between the content of the memory of the intellectual and political elite and the general public, as well as differences in the axiological orientations that influence memory. The results of the study presented in this chapter confirm these differences and therefore the limited influence of the elite on the vernacular memory. The memories of the elite and of the masses function in two distinct systems of values. Having better knowledge of history, the elites perceive contemporary politics of memory from the perspective of historical interpretations, which are dominated by conflictual narratives of the past and of Polish-German relations. However, there are also significant differences within this group regarding the attitude to commemorating the city's German past. In other social groups, the temperature of the dispute is lower but the idea of commemorating the city's German past is generally not widely accepted.

The power over memory has numerous cultural limitations in the form of the normative system that defines patterns of commemorative practices. Power that breaks accepted norms of commemoration may simply be ineffective. For instance, the institutionalisation of commemorative practices often transforms

---

28 Sennett analyses the influence of labour on the attitude to the past and the future. In digital business, which is focused on constant development of new products, the past is not valued whatsoever. The attitude to the past that is developed in work transfers into the private sphere: "my claim is that people do not remember well because the modern economy does not encourage it" (Sennett 2011:286).

spontaneous practice into dead rituals. The limitations also concern the scope of power. The power of the elite applies mostly to official memory. Official representations of history that are present in the public discourse can sometimes become dominant, as the example of the politics of memory in communist Poland demonstrates. However, there are also counter-memories, alternative versions of the past that contest the official picture. As a result of the dynamics of power-knowledge processes, some interpretations of history are marginalised and others become popular.

Rather than the power of the elite, collective memory is influenced by other processes, such as collective and personal experiences, which usually involve emotions. Although creating public events is in the hands of the elite, how the event is experienced and remembered cannot be completely controlled. The presented research on the reception of the politics of memory demonstrates that the influence of the political elite mostly applies to the intellectual elite who participate in the debates about memory. The general populace, on the other hand, remains outside this area of discourse – collective memory only includes fragmentary information, myths, stereotypes and clichés.

The case of Wrocław demonstrates social conditions in which the politics of memory, as a certain form of propaganda, can actually influence memory – as it was in the times of the Polish People's Republic. From the comparison of the communist and the post-communist politics of memory, one may conclude that the latter is less systematic and less effective. Moreover, it seems that contemporary politics of memory do not offer a new approach to history or a new attitude to past conflicts. Thus, in a sense, the politics of memory developed in the Polish People's Republic is still valid.

Grzegorz Kozdraś

To Leave a Trace on Urban Walls: Youth Cultures in the Third Circulation of Memory in the City

Abstract: Based on the theory of the circulation of culture, this chapter discusses a model of circulation of memory with reference to the power-memory relations in the city. Particular attention has been given to the circulation of the memory of marginalised groups, which, for cultural and structural reasons, are deprived of access to the circulations typical for the official public sphere. Youth subcultures are one of these groups. By creating *generational legends*, subcultures preserve the memory of their group, build its identity and strengthen integration processes as well as conquering and appropriating urban space.

Keywords: youth subcultures, collective memory, circulations of memory, city, appropriation

Introduction

Youth cultures are a subject of great interest to researchers from various academic disciplines. This phenomenon has been analysed from a historical perspective (Chabros 2014), a sociological perspective (Wrzesień 2013), a cultural studies perspective (Gelder 2007), a pedagogical perspective (Jędrzejewski 2001) and a psychological perspective (Piotrowski 2003). A number of works have been published that analysed selected youth subcultures: Bikini-boys[1] (Chłopek 2005), football fans (Dudała 2004), hackers (Jordan 2011) and hipsters (Litorowicz 2012). Youth culture has undergone general transformations and while subcultures have been in decline and are becoming gradually less radical (Wrzesień 2013: 7), they continue to fascinate.

The studies of youth subcultures relate to a wide variety of topics, including worldviews, systems of values, musical and ideological fascinations, the diversity of subcultures in the Polish People's Republic and their role in social change. Although research has shown that subcultures have history, the collective memory of subcultures is rarely a subject of study, with the exception of Barbara Fatyga's analysis (Fatyga 2005), which uses the category of time and space to describe

---

1 Polish: *Bikiniarze*

cultural experiences and that relates (collective) memory of subcultures to generational transmission of subcultural legends.

This chapter focuses on youth subcultures as actors in the process of social production of space and their participation in creating the memory of places through appropriation and symbolic annexation of space. Generally, however, rather than analysing the phenomenon of subcultures, this chapter deals with the memory of subcultures that emerges in spaces and places that are annexed, appropriated and personalised by these groups. Youth subcultures, as well as many other social actors, are often ignored in debates about memory and deprived of the right to commemorate their history in public space by contributing to its *information dress* (Wallis 1977). This process, however, does not completely remove subcultural memory from urban space; it only moves it into an area that may be described as a third circulation of memory.[2]

On the one hand, cities are utilitarian spaces of existence that allow residents to fulfil their needs. On the other, they are symbolic spaces filled with meanings; they are also carriers and creators of memory. As Aleksander Wallis noted, cities reflect the tastes, preferences, needs and lifestyles of their residents. They also influence their dwellers by "strengthening a particular set of values" and combining the past and the present within the urban space (Wallis 1979: 12–13). The past of a city is embedded in its "stone cityscape", walls and memorials. These settings maintain the balance between individual and collective memory (Benovolo 1995: 10). Inscriptions on walls are a special source of memory for a city (Grębowiec 2008). Urban walls are a space of preserving memory.

Studies on the social memory of cities have a long tradition (see Boyer 1996) and have increased dramatically in popularity in recent years. As Pierre Nora noted, this popularity results from a crisis of memory in contemporary societies that turn away from their past and look to the present and future in the name of progress (2009: 4). On the other hand, access to historical data and the high status of memory in the media result in the presence of memory in everyday life. Magdalena Saryusz-Wolska writes that "contemporary culture is flooded by both amnesia and obsessive remembering" (2011: 93).

According to Christine M. Boyer, the process of creating memory of a city, particularly in socially and culturally heterogeneous urban communities, creates certain problems. Memory of the city is selective, incoherent, fragmentary and dispersed (Boyer 1996). It is a product of a particular community of memory

---

2   The theory of the third circulation of memory refers to Jerzy Wertenstein-Żuławski's theory of three circulations of culture (1991).

(Nora 2009) and, most of all, it is entangled in power relations and produced "in the process of appropriating the city" (Saryusz-Wolska 2011: 101). "Memory and sites of memory are an effect of the intentional actions of certain social groups (e.g. the social elite)", Barbara Pabjan and Paweł Czajkowski note, referring to the works of Pierre Nora (Pabjan and Czajkowski 2015). Therefore, if urban residents can be defined as a heterogeneous community, how should the city's social memory, which is filled with diversity and tensions, be approached? Does access to common space allow all the groups of residents to express their memory and identity? Do all the residents have the right to the city, which, according to David Harvey, is "a right to change and reinvent the city more after our hearts' desire" (Harvey 2012: 4)? Thus, do they have a right to create memory in the urban space?

Let's leave a trace on urban walls – the *information dress* of Wrocław and its subcultural *patches*

Urban space can speak, Bohdan Jałowiecki notes (Jałowiecki 2002), but to understand its words it is necessary to know the code – the language that is embedded in material forms (Jałowiecki 2002). One of Aleksander Wallis's numerous important contributions to the theory of the social nature of cities was the concept of the *information dress of a city*. In his analysis of urban centres, Wallis used this theory to combine permanent elements of the urban tissue: architecture, layout, memorials and monuments, with temporary and everyday elements. The information dress serves a communicative and instrumental function. It also has a cognitive role that allows for a sense of direction in the urban space and in the city's history and that builds the memory of the city. Finally, it occupies an aesthetic role and an ideological role that involves cultural meanings embedded in urban space (Wallis 1997). The information dress expresses the values, lifestyles, and political and legal systems of societies, thus allowing for identification with a city and its social and functional structure (Ibid.).

"The Śląsk Wrocław football fans rapidly paint huge amounts of graffiti. Colourful images have already been created below the Gądowianka overpass, on Strzegomska street, in Bielany Wrocławskie, in Nowy Dwór and on Żmigrodzka street. All of them were based on project proposals and with the permission of the walls' owners", a local paper informs (Torz 2010). It is impossible to walk on the streets of Wrocław today without coming across a wall painting that glorifies the local football club. The sheer volume of these creations makes the public space of the city a gallery of their works.

Graffiti, paintings, murals and other products of the youth of Wrocław's subcultural activity cover the walls of many buildings and fences. As an important component of the local information dress, they can be found on bridges, viaducts, rubbish bins, trams and trains. Inscriptions on urban walls are the work of diverse youth groups and subcultures. They present the fascinations and ideologies of their creators, and they also include symbols that manifest their attitudes, feelings and beliefs. They describe events that are important for the subcultures and they commemorate subcultural heroes and saints. They manifest antipathy towards other subcultures or football fans who support other teams and towards the political power and system. Finally, they emphasise their current or future presence in the city's space.

The walls of Wrocław have long expressed the subcultural identity of the city's youth. Although it would be difficult to specify the first moment when graffiti appeared in public space, the 1980s were the time when graffiti became observable to an extent previously unknown. The times favoured the development of this phenomenon: on the one hand, the Carnival of Solidarity, the martial state and social resistance against the communist regime, on the other hand, developing counter culture, new wave and rock scene, and youth subcultures (Gregorowicz and Waloch 1991). Other phenomena should also be noted, such as environmental, anarchist and pacifist movements and other social movements that contested the communist system, like the Orange Alternative, which inspired the youth to create a variety of inscriptions and to paint slogans and graffiti using a template technique. This technique soon became a hallmark of Polish graffiti. As Ewa Chabros notes, a particular interest in templates as a method of tagging space was observable in the mid-1980s. Western graffiti was thought to express a rebellion "against the communist authorities as well as against the Polish reality of the time – young people criticized political life, social institutions, school and traditional values that were identified with family or the Catholic Church" (Chabros 2011: 211). According to the authors of *Graffiti w PRL* (*Graffiti in the Polish People's Republic*), graffiti was a tool for the excluded – their opportunity to oppose and express their own opinion in a public space. They also coloured the grey walls and brought smiles to pedestrians' faces (Chabros and Kmita 2011).

While at the beginning of the 1990s template graffiti became a mass phenomenon, it almost completely disappeared in the middle of this decade (Chabros 2011: 228). Political graffiti disappeared and an era of subcultural graffiti started. Templates were replaced with huge murals. Urban space became an area of competition for domination between different subcultural groups (Kozdraś 2006, 2011).

Football fans are a particularly noticeable group among many active youth subcultures (Dudała 2004, Miecik 2001). Dominik Antonowicz and Łukasz Wrzesiński (2009) call them a "community of invisible religion". Football fans are active in basically every city or town that has a football club and they symbolically appropriate public space. Different groups of football fans compete for the best and most effective mural (Torz 2010) and they attempt to conquer the space of other subcultures or groups of football fans. Through symbols located within it, public space becomes a site for expressing feelings, like pride, and the history of a club and its fans as well as aversion and hostility towards others, while walls become a site for expressing and preserving memory of events, places and people that are important for a group.

The metaphor of invisible religion that was used by Antonowicz and Wrzesiński accurately represents the *sacred* character of football fans' fascination, not only due to the depth of fans' fanaticism all over the world (Brown 2007), but also due to the symbolic value of club colours, the celebration of games, matchday choreography and commemoration of "martyrs" – the victims of the football's "holy war".[3] The organisation of football fans during away games, e.g. marches through cities accompanied by songs and chants, make fans resemble conquistadors who come to conquer another land (Sahaj 2012). Club stadiums, particularly in South America, are like temples and games resemble Holy Masses (Antonowicz and Wrzesiński 2009). A club's past is a special object of cult fixation – it is commemorated in scarves, graffiti, sticker art and murals, and the year when a club was founded is often displayed next to its name.

By creating a symbolic community and referring to a common universe of meanings – the name of the club, the colours (red, white and green), the crest and the date of the club's foundation (1947) – football fans in Wrocław (in particular the fans of WKS Śląsk Wrocław) create their places in the city and emphasise their association with the city and its past. The structure of their narrative that is formed in this way (Fatyga 2005) underlines the local character of their community. On the other hand, Wrocław fans (and fans from other cities, as internet forums of other clubs demonstrate) also use national symbols and refer to the national community.

The notion of subculture

Despite the vast number of academic works devoted to youth subcultures that have been published, sociological interest in this phenomenon is not decreasing.

---

3 The most popular example of commemorating the 'martyrs' of the football fan war is the plaque next to the main gate to Anfield that includes the names of the 96 Liverpool fans who died in 1989 at Hillsborough Stadium, Sheffield, during the 1988/1989 FA Cup semi-final.

While the studies of subcultures are rich and diverse, they lack conclusiveness regarding the fundamental problem of the definition of subcultures, particularly youth subcultures.

Depending on the approach, there are different ways of defining subcultures. There are many definitions of subcultures, but two general types. According to the first, a subculture is an element or a characteristic of a general culture (e.g. youth culture) while the other category of definitions relates subcultures to the characteristics of particular social groups.

The notion of subculture was introduced to sociology by M.M. Gordon, who used it to describe the relationship between minority groups' culture and the dominant culture (in this case, the national culture). Subculture is an outcome of social relations between the national (dominant) culture and the social position of individuals resulting from class, ethnic background, place of residence and religion (Siemaszko 1993: 134). Therefore, according to Gordon, subculture is an attribute of dominant culture that relates to the ways in which individuals or social groups learn and reinforce this culture.

Jerzy Wertenstein-Żuławski understands subculture as a set of cultural patterns that distinguish a group from society. These patterns, however, do not regulate the entire sphere of a group's activity but only some aspects of it, therefore they must be complemented by the patterns of dominant culture; in other words, norms that regulate activities other than subcultural activities. The author differentiates between subculture as defined above, counter-culture and alternative culture. Counter-culture is also a set of cultural patterns, but it covers the entire activity of a group that is in opposition to the dominant culture – without which counter-culture cannot exist. Dominant culture is *sin qua non* for counter-culture, as counter-culture defines itself through contrast with mainstream values. Alternative culture, on the other hand, is free from the "burden" of dominant culture as, according to the author, the former modifies some elements of the latter and enriches it by adding new elements. Alternative culture is a set of autonomous cultural rules and patterns (Wertenstein-Żuławski 1990: 9–10).

Referring to Wertenstein's and Żuławski's theory, Barbara Fatyga identifies youth subcultures with youth culture. She believes that almost all youth subcultures aim to create their own autonomous culture (alternative culture), thus they are in fact carriers of alternative culture (Fatyga 2005: 107–108). In this sense, youth as a social category is identical to subculture.

Unlike the abovementioned authors, Mirosław Pęczak defines subculture as a social group that is on the margins of "the patterns of social life that dominate in a social system" and that expresses its distinctness by undermining or denying commonly accepted and reinforced cultural patterns. In this approach, subcultural practices are constitutive elements of a social group (Pęczak 1992). Similarly, Claude S. Fischer believes that subcultures are almost all social groups of a "suitable" size that have a distinguishing lifestyle, and a system of values, norms and beliefs. According to Fischer, subcultures are elements of a larger social group or entire society, and the more complex the society, the more diverse the subcultures (Fischer 1975, 1995).

Jerzy Dudała, who studies football fans, refers to Konarski's definition. Konarski considers subculture a particular social group that is distinct from the general public and that expresses its distinctiveness in common interests and aspirations, exclusive norms and values, its own behaviour patterns, territorial, ethnic and religious bonds and its clearly defined lifestyle (Dudała 2004: 69).

In his work dedicated to intergenerational relations, Witold Wrzesień makes an effort to combine two ways of defining subcultures. In analysing the process of creating generational groups, the author points at subcultures as the fundamental element that constitutes a generation. In this context, Wrzesień understands subculture as a group that aims to create alternative culture and as a group of young people of a "specified time and place" who co-create the patterns of alternative culture (Wrzesień 2003: 47).

Deliberations on youth subcultures fit into the context of relations between the general, dominant culture (or a culture of the dominant group) and culture / cultures with a narrower range of influence, particularly the cultures of social minorities (Mucha 1999: 15, 21). According to this approach, there is a relatively coherent, general cultural pattern, within which subcultures emerge, usually in a spontaneous way (this process mostly applies to youth subcultures).

Appropriation, conquest and production of places – subcultures

The social and cultural heterogeneity of the residents of big cities provided a good basis for the emergence of various subcultural groups. This was the case in London, where, in the 1960s and the 1970s, the underground movement, which manifested the contestation and subcultural identity of the youth of London, developed more intensively than in other similar cities (Paleczny 1993). Underground activity is permanently embedded into the London city landscape (Muggleton 2004; Prus 2006). On the one hand, the underground enriched the cultural and social urban mosaic (Ibid.); on the other hand, it contributed to making citizens feel unsafe and to the devaluation of public space (Klein and Maxson 2006; Hagedorn 2007).

The activity of youth subcultures in urban space is often identified with symbolic appropriation of space. This phenomenon results from the territorial character of subcultural groups. They consider their closest living space an important part of their identity that should be protected by guarding boundaries and controlling the presence of others.

In sociology and other disciplines that deal with social space, appropriation and conquest are terms that usually express that the condition of the public space will be modified in such a way to make a specific group feel more at home, while simultaneously alienating others (Jałowiecki and Szczepański 2002; Hołyst 2007). To appropriate means to take possession of something, often unlawfully, or to give oneself the right to do something, while conquest is an action that aims to increase domination over a space. Generally, thus, appropriation of a space is an act of giving oneself the right to stay in an area or make use of it, while conquest of a space means gaining an advantage over other users of an area. Roberta Feldman and Susan Stall note that appropriation of a space is related to attitudes towards this space and define appropriation as "individuals' or groups' creation, choice, possession, modification, enhancement of, care for, and/or simply intentional use of a space to make it one's own" (Feldman and Stall 1994: 172).

Through appropriation, individuals or groups transform their physical environment into a meaningful place or, as Florian Znaniecki put it, they produce spatial value (Znaniecki 1938). Groups may thus "intentionally occupy the setting; possess, construct, modify, enhance or care for a physical setting; mark a setting with identifying signs, symbols, or activities; and/or simply represent a setting in words or images" (Feldman and Stall 2004: 185). The appropriated space is conceptualised as "an interactive process through which individuals purposefully transform the physical environment into a meaningful place while in turn transforming themselves" (Feldman and Stall 1994: 172).

Appropriation of space reveals the power to dominate and control parts of the city; it results in segregation, exclusion and limitation or lack of access to public space (and/or public places). In this sense, it expresses the practices of domination and power. On the other hand, it can also express social resistance to domination and power. According to Henri Lefebvre's analysis, social appropriation of space can also serve to regain public space. Thus, it manifests competition for space, expresses opposition to exclusionary tendencies and is a means of protest against the domination of the state and capital. Using Lefebvre's notion of *representational spaces*, one can demonstrate that through the practices of appropriation, defined as symbolic marking of a space, groups create their own, familiar space (Lefebvre 1990: 38).

The process of appropriation of space is twofold. On the one hand, in appropriating and conquering a space, social actors have the power to exercise control and impose the rules of desired or acceptable behaviour. An example of this type of appropriation, which is also empirically available, is beer gardens that restaurateurs set up in public spaces. Beer gardens are a persuasive way of taking possession of a space, which becomes cased, fortified and saturated with material tissue.

On the other hand, appropriation and conquest of a space may also relate to a process of making it familiar by saturating the spatial tissue with material and visual codes, signs and symbols that convey additional senses and meanings. It may also take place as a result of the permanent and systematic presence and activity of social groups in particular places. This type of appropriation is called symbolic or social appropriation and involves over-representation or excessive presence of some visual forms and content.

Appropriation of space may refer to the process of making it familiar. In this sense, appropriation is a process in which communities aim to explore a particular urban space, increase its value and identify it as safe (Jałowiecki and Szczepański 2002). It is a process of redefining a space that results from both planned and spontaneous activity by individuals and groups, users and owners of this space. It is also a process of generating subcultural memory. Not only does the process of appreciation create a meaningful space, it also generates memory and identity of places (see Jałowiecki 2002). The collective memory of groups is located in places, which, saturated with historical artefacts, create a narrative about the past and support weakening memory. Appropriated by subcultures, spaces become subcultural sites of memory, symbolic places, which, as Stefan Bednarek notes (2010), evoke memories and become an element of group identity.

The problem of collective memory and collective memory of subcultures

Social or collective memory is knowledge about a group and its past with reference to this past. As Marian Golka laconically – in his own words – defined it, "social memory is socially generated, transformed or unified knowledge about the past of a community" (Golka 2009: 15). This knowledge, which includes diverse content, "is acquired by individuals from different sources", is relatively unified and lasts thanks to oral messages as well as cultural products: those that are produced now and that consolidate people's knowledge and those from the past that symbolise what is important for a community (Ibid.: 15).

Sociology and other academic disciplines owe the term *collective memory* to Maurice Halbwachs and his canonical work *On Collective Memory*. Halbwachs believed that individual memories are socially generated and socially embedded. Different social frameworks in which people exist determine their recollections, making them similar to the recollections of others. As Halbwachs put it: "it is in society that people normally acquire their memories. It is also in society that they recall, reorganise, and localize their memories" (Halbwachs 1992: 38). As people exist as part of social groups, individual memory is also the collective memory of a group. On the other hand, it is contextual and depends upon individual contexts.

Maurice Halbwachs' notion of collective memory was creatively expanded upon, both in Poland (see Kończal and Wawrzyniak 2011) and elsewhere. This memory boom was institutionalised in the form of the growing area of memory studies. Terms similar to collective memory were coined, such as social memory or cultural memory (and a rich variety of other notions and theories, see Saryusz-Wolska and Traba 2014).

Referring to Yuri Lotman's and Boris Uspensky's definition of culture as the non-inheritable memory of a collective, Aleida Assmann develops the concept of cultural memory, which is an overall frame for culture-making processes. It includes accumulating the memory of the past of a community (*storage-memory*) as well as preserving material traces of the cultural past and selecting objects or knowledge from the reservoir of cultural artefacts (*function-memory*) that continue to draw attention thanks to their power of expression (Assmann 2013: 54–57; Saryusz-Wolska 2014: 337–338). In this sense, cultural memory is a quintessence, a final stadium or form of collective memory.

According to Assmann, collective memory is not a social construct. Social groups and institutions do not *have* memory; they *create* it using signs, symbols, texts, images, rituals and practices. By doing so, they transmit particular messages to individuals, "making them carriers of collective memory" and they constitute their own, collective identity. The construction of collective memory makes it coherent and clear. It confronts other collective memories and is based on symbols that "unify and generalise memories" (Assmann, idem: 48–49). It serves to transfer knowledge and memories to the next generations and it gains its stability using "dense content, intensification of symbols" and basing its foundations on strong emotions. The trouble with collective memory is its unification and politicisation (Ibid.: 56). It is an element of shaping the politics of memory.

In his analysis of the democratisation of collective memory, Marek Ziółkowski assumed a pluralistic character for collective memory in a democratic society. The essence of this pluralism is to recognise different perspectives on the past and create conditions for unrestricted and equal articulation of opinions. Working on this assumption, Ziółkowski defined collective memory as a "set (system) of beliefs about the past that are part of social consciousness, in which individual memories intermingle with messages received from other people" (Ziółkowski 2001: 3–4). According to this theory, collective memory relates to the common past of a group, it is perceived by the group as shared and it accompanies common actions (Ibid.: 4). Evoking collective memories always involves the expression of particular interests and the values of particular social actors who take part in the memory game between the state and its entities, institutions of civil society, non-institutionalised actors and external entities (Ibid.: 7). On the one hand, the stakes in this game are collective identity and belonging to the community; on the other, they are specific, particular interests. The more inequalities, privileges, suffering or injustice inherited by future generations, the stronger the need to articulate memory (Ibid.: 9).

Subcultural memory was perceived from the perspective of collective memory and it was not distinguished as a separate subject of analysis. While there is rich literature on memory about subcultures, subcultural and counter-cultural activity and the history of this activity (see Chabros 2014), written also by former participants in such groups (e.g. Frydrych 2002), subcultural memory has not yet been analysed. While it is sometimes used when describing the mechanisms of the relations between members of subcultures or their ideologies (see Petrova 2006), the term is not defined or explained, with the exception of Barbara Fatyga's work *Dzicy z naszej ulicy*, in which the author deals with the subject of the role of memory in the process of constituting generational communities. It should be emphasised that the author does not use the term *subcultural memory* but *generational legend*.

A generation is formed on the basis of a community of generational experiences. They are a reference point for the social achievements of an individual. Based on attitudes to generational experiences and the ability to create a narrative about these experiences, the author distinguishes a narrower and broader meaning of the term *generation*. In the former sense, a generation is a group of people of similar social status who form a community of experience; generational legend (a story about these experiences) can be used to exercise power similar to Bourdieu's *symbolic violence*. In the latter, broader sense, a generation is an anonymous community of people who identify only with some experiences: "selected elements of worldview, certain types of behaviour, language, fashion, music or stereotypes that have been created by this community or by the general public" (Fatyga 2005: 152). This generational community adopts fragments of the generational legend.

Generational legend is the main carrier of subcultural memory; it is a form of cultural transmission. It combines elements of individual narratives, individual memories, which become general subcultural memory. With the passage of time or as a result of other factors, this memory is subject to change and modification. One of the important factors of modification is the mechanism of cultural forgetting or hypertrophy of memory (Ibid.: 156). It is a result of individual biographical work. Viewing the legend in the light of their personal experiences, individuals modify the legend, which then becomes mythicised and acquires new meaning for the carriers of memory (Ibid.: 157). Without being strengthened by other sources, the collective memory of youth subcultures is very short, as Barbara Fatyga notes. Permanent rotation of members of subcultural groups does not help to "create generational symbols" (Fatyga 2005: 158). Additionally, the problem of subcultural memory relates to the mechanism of its transition. Subcultural memory rarely becomes an element of the broader, dominant community's memory. It is rather an element of the third circulation of culture.

Third circulation of culture – third circulation of memory

Activities that relate to the first, second and third circulation structures involve relations between the official and legal and the unofficial and/or illegal. In the Polish People's Republic, the second and third circulations were non-system channels of distributing information and goods, including culture and memory. According to Barbara Fatyga, the role of the third circulation of culture should be perceived from the perspective of communication.

> This perspective focuses on the circulation of cultural content between different groups. It is also important that in each of the distinguished circulations the content circulates from a particular kind of sender to a particular kind of recipient and, at least in some respects, specific communication channels. These elements constitute communication situations that should also acknowledge (e.g. differentiate, depending on a circulation) contexts of sending, transfer and reception, the cultural competences of senders and recipients and types of messages (cultural texts) that are specific for each circulation (Fatyga 2005: 110).

According to Janusz Lalewicz, the theory of circulation of culture relates to activities that, in the communication process, connect all the participants, recipients and creators of this process as well as its cultural products. The theory describes the process of transmission and storage of the content of cultural activity (Lalewicz 1985). Considering that the main subject of Lalewicz's interest was literature, the author defines the process or act of communication as a set of conditions for formulating and interpreting literary texts that is determined by the system of recipients and senders and transmission techniques that include the method of transmission, the medium and the communication network (Lalewicz 1975: 73–74).

Today, *circulations of culture* is a term that is used in studies of underground, counter-cultural, subcultural and alternative creativity and activity in the Polish People's Republic as well as in the analysis of illegal distribution of cultural content, particularly with the use of contemporary media such as the internet and mobile phones (see Filiciak, Hofmokl and Tarkowski 2012).

The theory of three circulations of culture concerns the phenomenon of independent, unofficial culture in communist Poland that was in opposition to mainstream culture and its distribution channels. The first circulation referred to the official, dominant culture, sometimes defined as high culture and sometimes even as popular culture (Ibid.: 111). Only after it was censored was the content distributed through official channels. The second circulation, as Jerzy Wertenstein-Żuławski notes (1991: 225, after Fatyga 2005: 111), was in opposition to the first; "it was created by people from the Solidarity movement and other groups that opposed censorship and regulations that limited and controlled the distribution of information". According to Mirosław Pęczak (1988), in addition to manifesting opposition to the regime, the second circulation complemented the first. For the most part, the phenomenon of the second circulation of culture, i.e. specifically the Polish underground press,[4] resulted from the censorship of anti-system academic and literary works (Supruniuk and Supruniuk 2015). As Pęczak (1991: 204) put it, the second circulation became "the voice of those who cannot express their opinions and beliefs using the official media".

The third circulation of culture was an alternative to the first two. It rejected the official, first circulation culture, accusing it of having a commercial character and promoting a consumerist lifestyle. It was intended as a manifestation of resistance against the culture of adults and official politics. At the beginning, the third circulation was similar to the second in its assumptions. However, with transformations in the political opposition, differences emerged that led to a clear separation of the third circulation as an autonomous subsystem of culture (Fatyga 2005: 111–112).

The third circulation provided space for youth culture to emerge spontaneously, communicate and manifest their attitudes. It is important from the perspective of communication that it was an inter-subcultural medium that transmitted patterns of behaviour, attitudes, opinions and beliefs. While the fact that oppositional activity centred around the second circulation was a particular subject of interest to the authorities (see Supruniuk and Supruniuk 2015), the third circulation was

---

4 As noted in *Drugi obieg wydawniczy (1974) 1976–1990 w zasobie biblioteki uniwersyteckiej w Toruniu*, independent publications distributed in communist countries were called *Samizdat* in Western Europe.

tolerated by them. According to Jerzy Wertenstein-Żuławski (1991), this tolerance was a method to prevent a youth revolt.

Mirosław Pęczak (1991) associates the phenomenon of second and third circulation with Robert White's theory of alternative communication, which he contrasts with dominant communication. Referring to Louis Althusser's theory, dominant communication is one of the ideological state apparatuses. Thanks to this apparatus, the state maintains control over the form and content of communication and ensures the reproduction of the state ideology (see Althusser 2006). The ideological character of dominant communication also manifests itself through popular culture. As a result, the status of culture and its consumption changes and the ideologisation of culture enters the sphere of everyday life (Pęczak 1991: 200). As Gramsci notes (1968), by using popular culture, dominant culture strengthens the hegemony of the ruling class, thus serving to maintain the worldview and power of dominant social groups.

Marginalised groups respond to the dominant, official communication by claiming their right to participate in the cultural system and demanding democratisation of the communication system (White 1985 quoted in Pęczak 1991). As Pęczak (1991: 204) notes:

> Alternative communication today is introduced by marginalised groups in these [developed] societies. In principle, these groups either reject dominant patterns or their cultural deprivation results directly from social stratification. Their striving for emancipation and subjectivity makes them realise their goals through alternative, unconventional forms of expression and communication (…). This process can be defined as an attempt to eliminate alienation in the field of communication.

Alternative communication and culture do not always negate or reject the entire dominant communication and culture, as the second and third circulation demonstrate. Pęczak believes that the second circulation is only partially alternative to the dominant communication: it gives voice to those who would not otherwise have an opportunity to express their views. While it is a communication channel of the opposition, it does not promote values and patterns that are entirely in opposition to the dominant culture. Instead, it supplements the dominant culture and communication or is even subordinate to them. As Pęczak (1991: 205) notes:

> Texts distributed in the second circulation do not aim at revolution in behavioural patterns or dominating aesthetic tastes. In their artistic and, to some extent, ideological aspects (excluding the sharpening of political accents), belles-lettres published by independent publishers remain the same as they were in times of their official status in the canon of high culture.

Rather than rejecting social norms and values, the second circulation accepts them, thus it supplements the official, dominant culture and influences it. Hence, activity in the second circulation does not question traditional patterns of family life, socialisation, religiousness and other patterns (Ibid.: 206).

The third circulation, according to Barbara Fatyga, was characterised by negation and distance from the official and dominant culture. It was a medium and an expression of contestation. What is more, it fully implemented the ideological principles of the youth subcultures and counter-cultures of the 1980s and the 1990s that often referred to the slogan Do It Yourself. More importantly, it helped circulate and transmit subcultural ideas, attitudes, values and norms as well as subcultural, collective memory.

Knowledge is inextricably related to power, as Foucault wrote (1975). According to the French philosopher, power permeates the entire sphere of social relations and it cannot be reduced to centralising institutions, judgement or law. Power manifests itself in discourse and through discourse. Discourse establishes and defines object domains for knowledge and excludes other forms of knowledge as improper or incomprehensible. It provides ways of thinking and speaking about certain subjects by repeating certain ideas, practices and forms of knowledge. It also regulates who can speak, when and in what circumstances. This way, the power-knowledge constructs the regime of truth.

Memory is power, George Orwell noted in his work *Nineteen Eighty-Four*: "Who controls the past (…), controls the future: who controls the present controls the past" (Orwell 1977: 34). Jacek Nowak (2001) states that collective memory emerges as a result of three factors: "tradition, memory makers and memory consumers". The first defines the ways of presenting the past, the second consists of categories that filter and select memory, and the third defines which users of memory can ignore it, acquire it or modify it for their own needs. The process of recollecting memory is a kind of a game between society and its representatives, friendship circles (informal institutions) and the media.

Marek Ziółkowski notes that, in the Polish People's Republic, there were basically two players in this game – the authorities and society – and memory was transmitted in one direction only, from the former to the latter. Having a monopoly on memory, the authorities (or their special institutions: memory makers) distributed memory in the first circulation by manipulating and deciding what should be remembered and what should be forgotten. The first circulation is a channel of transmitting official memory (tradition, in Ziółkowski's terms). However, it is also a field (in Bourdieu's terms) of struggle over the official, dominant memory that lays claims to possess cultural memory (in Assmann's terms). Memory distributed in the first circulation is expected to legitimise and consolidate power by creating images that emphasise the historical role of the authorities, their relationship with society and the involvement of other actors in creating memory in accordance with official memory. The first circulation also removes certain memories or their elements. When creating first-circulation memory, the authorities refer to social myths, stereotypes and prejudices (Nowak 2011).

As mentioned above, the first circulation of memory is a field of struggle for access to the official memory. Consumers of memory can acquire, process or contest the officially distributed memory according to the level of inequality and the sense of injustice related to the past and having influence on the present. The sense of injustice and inequality is to some extent related to the sense of belonging to a group and opposition to other groups (Ziółkowski 2001: 9–10). If it cannot be overcome, the alternative, oppositional memory distributed in the second circulation remains.

Second circulation of memory is mostly instrumental memory that is used by groups that are or feel marginalised to create, consolidate and legitimise their claims. These claims involve the factors that cause the sense of injustice and inequality. Thus, the memory of the second circulation aspires to occupy a position in the first circulation either by displacing the dominant memory or (in democratic systems) by incorporating alternative memory into the field of official memory.

The memory of the second circulation reproduces all the factors that constitute the memory of the first circulation. Using Jacek Nowak's terminology, it uses the same traditions, i.e. ways of talking about the past, the same memory makers, i.e. professionals dealing with the past, and it addresses memory to the same consumers. For this reason, it is often used by the political opposition and marginalised groups to manifest their claims.

The third circulation stems from resistance to the first as well as from a misunderstanding and a lack of acceptance of the second, particularly regarding the claims made by marginalised groups that want to enter the first circulation. It is thus a manifestation of these groups' agency. The third circulation also results from certain structural and cultural barriers. They are related to the lack of space to manifest interests and needs that are different from dominant and oppositional ones, particularly when they clearly contradict dominant narratives and oppositional claims (Fatyga 2005; Pęczak 1991, 2013). Thus, the third circulation provides a framework for groups that oppose the status quo to communicate their needs and claims as well as to consolidate their memory.

In the third circulation of memory, social groups use instruments of creating memory that imitate the second circulation as well as those that are not used in it due to their illegal character. Thus, subcultural groups are active in the third circulation beyond the legal sphere or by using illegal methods such as creating graffiti, murals and inscriptions in public spaces.

Iwona Borowik

Transformation of Architectural Space in Wrocław

Abstract: This chapter describes urban public space as an area of conflict and coopera-tion. It presents the significance of architecture and its influence on the public space of a post-Fordist (post-socialist) city, with focus on the example of Wrocław. Architecture is defined as a material and a component of a new socio-spatial order, as an urban symbolic regime, and a new ideology of urban space.

Keywords: socio-spatial order, architecture and architectural space, socialist and post-socialist city, ideology

Introduction

Contemporary Polish cities have been undergoing an advanced process of change – from a period of strongly ideologised socialism (1945–1989) into a phase of a post-Fordism (post-socialism) that is subordinated to the ideology of the free market and consumption. The many social, cultural, economic or aesthetic consequences resulting from this process are being observed by sociologists. Wrocław, one of the biggest and most beautiful Polish cities, called the Venice of the North, is an exemplification of these global changes in the architectural space of Polish cities. A metropolitan area – on a Polish scale – Wrocław prides itself on its long history and multicultural heritage as well as an excellent geographical and geopolitical location in East-Central Europe. Inhabited by 600,000 residents, it is a capital of one of the most beautiful European regions: Lower Silesia. Rich history and tradi-tion, old architecture, but also socialist concrete combined with capitalist glass and particularism constitute the architectural space of Wrocław. This chapter will focus on the architectural aspect of the urban space, defining architecture as material and an element of the socio-spatial organisation of the city and a manifestation of the ideology of urban space that is dominant at a particular time. By characterising two phases of urbanist development of Wrocław, the chapter will, using Wrocław as an example, demonstrate the nature and extent of changes that have occurred in Polish post-socialist cities, with focus on elements of its architecture and urban planning: the postmodern department store *Solpol* (1993), the only skyscraper in the city, *Sky Tower* (2010) and a model housing estate *Nowe Żerniki* (2016).

Architecture and architectural space

The factor that determines the cultural value and universal character of a city is the identity of architectural and public space based on the mainstays of persistence, continuance and syncretism as well as classical and humanistic values (the Vitruvius's principles: *utilitas, firmitas* and *venustas*, translated as functionality, solidity and beauty). The character of a city, the perception of its urban intentional landscape, or the image of a city in the mind's eye of its residents and users are influenced by the city's physical and cultural manifestation, i.e. its architectural-urban form. This form reveals itself and can be perceived mostly in the collective space of social interactions and in the human-space interaction. It is collectively used and experienced and a sense of community is built within it. Its perception as the symbol of a city, or, metaphorically, a visiting card, creates a sense of belonging, identification and satisfaction. As Leon Krier (2011) notes, referring to Hannah Arendt, public space can even be immortal. More importantly, however, it should be authentic (Zukin 2010), embedded in a specific cultural context and comprehensible within this context.

Performing a practical, functional role and connected with people more than any other form of art, architecture and urban planning express human ideas and values in every phase of social development. Architecture, in particular, is symbolically and materially significant, as it creates an individual and collective human environment and influences its quality. Like a lens, architecture focuses various human needs, expectations and aspirations. In a contemporary society in which nature and space have been conquered and dominated by human activity, culture and civilisation, architecture has become one of the most important human creations, as it externalises and embodies the living environment that has been shaped by cultural and social factors. In other words, it provides shelter and security, expresses social status, provides aesthetic sensations, and organises space in every context of the life of individuals and communities. Visible mostly in cities and their public space, architecture constitutes their cultural (intentional) landscape. Not only does it create individual spaces, it most of all produces public spaces that are jointly and collectively used. At the same time, it is subjectively valorised and socially objectified. According to Christian Norberg-Schulz's theory (1971: 37), architectural space is a concretisation of existential space.

The consistency and clarity of an architectural work of art consist of two main structural elements, namely form and function (i.e. content). This dualism should be harmonious, integral and complementary. It is important to find balance and moderation in the relation between form and content, to avoid the triumph of form over substance, or cover over content, which characterises, for example, architectural products of the contemporary culture of spectacle, eclectic historicism and postmodernism, as well as the triumph of content over form that was typical for socialist architecture. Otherwise, a simulated, ostensible, copied space with no connection to the natural and cultural environment will emerge and grow; inauthentic and artificial, it will not create a place. In the case of Wrocław, clear examples of this phenomenon are the large socialist housing complexes and the contemporary skyscraper *Sky Tower*, which will be discussed in detail later.

Architecture is an applied art, thus it should inspire and encourage a search for beauty/aesthetical values, it also should shape tastes and aesthetic awareness, express lifestyles and search for new trends in housing. Yet, it should not be too spontaneous, arrogant or overconfident in doing so, but let sociological knowledge support the creative process instead of repeating after Le Corbusier that it is life that is right and the architect who is wrong. People may not have knowledge or competence to appreciate an architectural work or the awareness of what they demand from architecture. This does not mean however, that their needs, expectations and aspirations can be ignored. Architecture should adapt to the changing cultural context, while also being a cicerone that leads towards new thinking about cultural space and its creation. These hopes have accompanied me since the concept of a model Wrocław housing estate *Nowe Żerniki*, planned as a continuation or link to the modernist WUWA from 1929 (Urbanik 2009).

Ideologies, architecture and the city. Perfect cities

Ideology is defined in this chapter as a set of coherent ideas, opinions and beliefs about the reality that also describe it. Although they are different, ideologies have one common feature: they are used, particularly by the authorities, to exert influence and pressure, to persuade individuals and groups to gain a particular perspective of the social world. With its incredible scale, elaboration and aspiration to be timeless, monumental architecture is a clear manifestation of ideology. It results from the belief of the (totalitarian) authority that political power will speak most forcefully through architecture (Nawratek 2005). Medieval temples and castles, the cities of Peter the Great, Stalin or Mussolini, skyscrapers and apartment blocks (not only socialist) demonstrate this phenomenon. After the fantastic modernism of the 1920s, Wrocław unfortunately experienced two architectural periods, one after another, which, although ideologically different, were similar in their consequences. They both brought monumentalism, spatial and cultural arrogance and symbolic violence (in Pierre Bourdieu's terms). One of them was the rule of the Third Reich and the chief architect Albert Speer, and the other, the post-war socialist realism and the socialist, crude version of modernism.

An analysis of ideologisation of space should include conceptualisations and visions of ideal cities that have been particularly significant for the architecture of the 20th and 21st century, i.e. those presented in the Athens Charter, *La Carta di Megaride*, the Leipzig Charter, the Charter of the New Urbanism and other documents. The principles of the Functional City postulated in the Athens Charter in 1933 have changed cities. In particular, they have influenced socio-spatial organisation of cities behind the Iron Curtain. According to Lewis Mumford, an expert in urban history, "an ideal city is a symbol of the most perfect organisation of space from the perspective of a certain epoch or an idealised image of a contemporary city" (Paszkowski 2011: 19). As Zbigniew Paszkowski adds, in the contemporary context "ideal city is understood as a certain challenge to create a perfect living environment for people. This environment should meet the needs of an individual person – a resident, as well as a collective that constitutes a particular urban, local and regional community" (Paszkowski 2011: 19). Confronted with reality, cities that were planned to be perfect rarely proved to be perfect; either the designer's ideas were not implemented or the project was not even launched. Nevertheless, the concepts of ideal cities are very significant for the development of European culture and civilisation, the ways of thinking about space and dwelling, and, specifically, for the development of architecture and urban planning. Today, ideal cities can be defined as those that are "designed according to a coherent urbanistic theory, to a cohesive project that reflects a particular philosophy of creating urban space" (Paszkowski 2011: 20).

Characteristics of the architectural space of socialist cities

The organisation and structure of socialist Polish cities from before the free election and political transition of 1989 were determined by many factors, primarily subordination to industry, nationalisation, lack of land rent or private property, and the domination of public interest over private interest. The totalitarian political power was manifested by architecture and symbolised by its monumetalism. Polish socialist cities were built mostly from ideological motives, based on universalistic postulates of the Functional City from the Athens Charter of 1933 (which rejected individualism and the prevailing model of a 19th century capitalist town) and a defined system of social, existential and aesthetic values. Additionally, war destruction, housing shortage, and the pressure of intensified industrialisation and urbanisation of the country resulted in the necessity of building as much as possible: fast, cheap, in mass, homogeneously and uniformly. Cities became functionalist machines to live in, work in and manifest support for the regime. Ideologically justified social egalitarianism, social homogenisation and the averaging of social needs influenced housing architecture. Housing norms were introduced that determined the maximum number of square meters of a living area per person and per family of a particular size. Socialist design and construction of housing lost the human factor, cultural and spatial context and local specificity. Widespread multi-family units, built of large concrete slabs arranged in monotonous, unified, large residential complexes, which were sometimes even inhabited by thousands of residents, dominated the urban landscape, being an architectural manifestation of the power of dominant ideology and public interest. Architecture was in most part total, deprived of style and character, trashy and ugly, amorphous and incapable of creating a place, i.e. identity, familiarity and closeness. Due to the lack of individual spaces that might provide intimacy (flats were tiny and homogeneous) the authorities forced social contacts and integration, i.e., the adaptation of socialist values. Residents and users of the city, however, should be free to decide on their own whether they want to unite or be separate, and architecture's only role should be to help them in their pursuits.

Wrocław broadened its administrative area in 1951 and 1973 but the city centre was not fully rebuilt or restored over the course of the period of socialism and remains incomplete to this day. The authorities focused on constructing residential complexes and housing estates – more than ten were built. The estates from the late 1950s and early 1960s were the most attractive from an architectural and social perspective (Gabiś 2011). The later they were built, the more unfriendly the scale, the weaker the architecture and the more mistakes were made in the decorative details and in the infrastructure. Generally, in the socialist period, Wrocław was spared excessive cultural and social homogenisation, but it experienced spatial and architectural uniformity. All in all, Polish cities were expected to be socially, culturally and architecturally similar. Fortunately, from time to time, buildings were also constructed that proved that decent architecture did not entirely disappear from Wrocław (e.g. *Trzonolinowiec* in Kościuszki Street, the residential towers at the Grunwaldzki Bridge, the residential and commercial building in Kołłątaja Street). Wrocław was also the first and perhaps the only Polish city that introduced infills to its spatial organisation on a considerable scale. The phenomenon of infills (the use of empty space between buildings for further construction, completing a frontline), initiated in the 1980s, was a salvation for the central areas of Wrocław from a housing, social, but also architectural and aesthetic point of view. This was a *specialite de la maison* of Wrocław on a national scale. The infills were a bridge between two epochs: the socialist and the capitalist, and between the modern and postmodern period. They were an urbanist catalysis and a form of gentrification; they expressed a turn to individualised and dedicated architecture. The more the 1990s progressed and the greater the increase in prices of urban land, the more the infills changed their character from strictly residential to commercial (services or offices). In this decade, freedom and democratisation of space consolidated, resulting in the development of the city, changes in the ownership of land and buildings (domination of banks) and postmodern architecture, diverse in terms of form and content, as exemplified by the unique and exceptional *Solpol*.

Solpol – almost the youngest postmodern monument in Wrocław

At the beginning of the 1990s, i.e. the period of political transition in Poland, the first private department store *Solpol* became an exceptional, even shocking, but also iconic building in Wrocław. It was opened in December 1993 in Świdnicka Street, which leads to the Old Market and is one of the oldest shopping streets in Wrocław. Built on the verge of two epochs, it became the city's only symbol of postmodern architecture, which was fashionable at the time. The expressive colours and controversial appearance and location of the building designed by Wojciech Jarząbek, when surrounded by the greyness of Wrocław public space, disturbed the harmony perceived by the residents and architects. It was integrated into an architectural sequence together with some of Wrocław's more eye-catching monuments: the gothic church of St. Dorothy, the neo-baroque building of the Monopol hotel and the neoclassical building of the Wrocław Opera. Yet it did not block out any of the historically significant buildings, while in later years the new architecture often overwhelmed other buildings and did not harmoniously fit into the existing urban environment.

Photograph 1: Solpol Department Store built in 1992–1993. Designed by Wojciech Jarząbek, Ar-5 Architectural Studio.

Source: http://blogi.wroclaw.pl

Solpol was so different from anything else that had been built in Wrocław for the previous forty years that controversy was inevitable. To some, e.g. the city officials, the conservator and the city architect, *Solpol* was beautiful, modern, visually attractive and perfectly integrated into the existing urban fabric. In the eyes of others, it embodied the kitsch and shoddiness of contemporary architecture and contrasted too much with the surroundings.

When larger shopping centres and modern office and apartment buildings started to appear in the urban space, *Solpol* lost its controversial character. When it turned out that the owner wanted to demolish the building, a social action was taken to save it and recognise its cultural and architectural value and list it as a protected monument. Yet, instead of becoming the youngest monument of postmodernism in Wrocław, *Solpol* will be destroyed. It seems neither sufficiently significant nor stylistically and architecturally strong to permanently co-create the structure of the urban public space and become a permanent element of the residents' consciousness. It will, however, remain a symbol of change in the urban space of Wrocław, as it was the first serious investment by a private investor in the very centre of a post-socialist city and was the first building to break the stereotypical and conventional spatial-architectural order. Moreover, what is important from a sociological perspective is that it has contributed to the transformation of social perception of urban and architectural space, i.e. a more reflexive and sensitive opening to the surrounding space and architecture, the awakening of architectural awareness.

A post-socialist city and its architectural space

As Polish cities became capitalist and postmodern, the old socialist ideology was considered to be *passé*, and Poles started to feel ashamed of Poland's architectural manifestation (e.g. grey, concrete blocks of flats, huge housing complexes, cheap trading pavilions). After years of shortages of various goods, including building materials, their production and demand for them began to increase, and new materials appeared that offered new possibilities for architecture and construction. "Little by little, building opportunities were rising, including the use of computer technology in design. The demand for shopping centres, cinemas, swimming pools, offices, warehouses and hotels increased. Foreign firms started to participate in the process of constructing new buildings (…) they brought in capital, but they also made demands that enforced good workmanship" (Czerner 2011: 133). Urban space in new cities, dominated by economical rather than political ideology, is increasingly privatised. Economic power continues to manifest itself in the size (height) and prestige of the architecture. Local authorities mostly decide the shape and quality of urban public space[1], which was particularly noticeable in the early period of the infatuation with the power of money during the transition of Polish cities in the 1990s. The priority of local authorities at the time was to find the easiest and, in their opinion, the best solution for the city budget and development. As a result, they treated the city as a growth machine. Thoughtless, short-sighted privatisation resulted in the sale of land to private investors and the creation of an urban regime of local and supra-local real estate business. Squandering the public space of Polish post-socialist cities and its progressive division brought further decentralisation, decomposition, deconstruction, fragmentation, decontextualisation and illegibility of urban space. The scattering of the city was aggravated by intensifying urban sprawl and the zoning of office buildings, housing estates and individual buildings (Gzell 2009).

The 21st century saw a renewal of Polish cities in the form of urban catalysis and revitalisation initiated by the municipal authorities (and which are now advanced in Wrocław), as well as gradual domestication and adaptation of alternative ways of thinking and creating urban space and cohabitation, for example, the idea of

---

1   The local government structure was rebuilt after 1989.

new urbanism, *smart city* or *slow city* as opposed to a "business and real estate-centred, profit-oriented model of rapid urban development of new districts and entire cities" (Paszkowski 2011: 13). However, contextually and architectonically unsuccessful projects were also developed, such as the only skyscraper in Wrocław, the *Sky Tower*. Unfortunately, this type of architecture increases the process of space defragmentation in contemporary Wrocław even more than socialist modernism.

Sky Tower – the skyscraper in Wrocław

An example of an event that contributed to the fragmentation and dispersion of Wrocław urban space was the permission granted by the local authorities to LC CORP for the construction of the tallest building in Poland – the 212-storey, multifunctional skyscraper *Sky Tower*.

Photograph 2: Sky Tower – the tallest multifunctional skyscraper in Poland, built 2007–2012. Designed by Walas Architectural Studio.

Source: http://wroclaw.dolny-slask.org.pl/

Sky Tower is actually a complex of three buildings of diverse size and form, located in the southern part of the city in the quarter of the Powstańców Śląskich, Wielka, Gwiaździsta and Szczęśliwa streets and opened in 2012 (when the UEFA European Championship took place, also in Wrocław). Unfortunately, the complex disrupted the existing spatial order and its readability. Jutting out alone, it does not create or highlight any social, spatial, cultural or aesthetic functions of this area of the city. Perhaps, if it co-created a complex of skyscrapers – an open, balanced and multifunctional district (in the form of a modern central business district) reflecting the metropolitan character of Wrocław, the perception of its form and function in newly developing public space would be more positive. Now, it is like a square peg in a round hole in the Wrocław architectural order that spoils the scale and intentional landscape of the capital of Lower Silesia with its shape and megalomaniacal and ostentatious size. Like *Solpol, Sky Tower* has provoked controversy and sparked off a public debate among residents and experts. It symbolises the confusion of the local authorities in their competition with other cities for capital, major events (the aforementioned EURO 2012) and tourists. It is also a manifestation of the attempts to find an architectural showcase and a prestigious symbol of the city at any cost. How, however, can this building signify prestige if it is commonly seen as a ridiculous phallic symbol? Although it has become a tourist attraction, particularly since the viewing platform was opened on the top, 49th floor, it is not perceived as an architectural masterpiece or a consistent element of the urban structure.

Urban space in post-socialist countries has been dominated by services, cultural industry, consumption and consumerism and the ludic culture of spectacle. As for architectural space and postmodernism, in the 1980s and the 1990s Europe returned to the "idea of the historic city with its compact buildings, frontage, built-up streets, squares and eclecticism of architectural forms" (Paszkowski 2011: 12). Wrocław also implemented these ideas and the aforementioned postmodernist department store *Solpol* was constructed for a private investor. However, Polish architectural space, including that in Wrocław, continues to be characterised by chaos and going from one extreme to the other: rejection of socialist architecture (although young Poles are beginning to appreciate the urban planning of socialist housing estates) and uncritical praise of contemporary architecture (related to the low aesthetic and architectural awareness of Poles). Yet, the golden mean should always be the priority, including the composition of space in modern cities. Balance between what is old and new, what should be rejected and what should be preserved and how to combine these elements in a harmonious and beautiful way is crucial. Nowadays one experiences the syndrome of excessive ambiguity, multi-contextuality, multi-functionality, indeterminacy, kitsch and ephemerality, which are characteristics of a consumer society. As Zbigniew Paszkowski (2011: 11) aptly notes,

> The solutions that are offered in the period of transition are most often functionalist and, deprived of ideological foundation, they are far from any idealism. Economic

pragmatism, speculative building, individual solutions that ignore citywide context and the perspective of urban development often result in urbanised spaces that are deprived of a coherent idea or creative expression. They are sometimes even detrimental to the further development of the city. The knowledge of ideal cities and the concepts behind them provides reflection on contemporary urbanistic problems. It is worth noting that utopian ideas have had an incredibly profound influence on urbanist creations over centuries, and, consequently, on the contemporary shape of cities that are a result of the implementation of these ideas. Nowadays, new concepts of ideal city structures are also formulated and there are attempts to improve the situation of existing cities.

In this respect, Wrocław has wonderful, experimental and visionary traditions (thanks to Max Berg, the city architect from 1909 to 1925), such as the *Home and Workplace* exhibition from 1929 (*Wohnung und Werkraum*, abbreviated WUWA). A desire to return to this tradition was expressed but the attempts were rather unsuccessful in terms of vision and organisation. On the occasion of promoting Wrocław as the European Capital of Culture 2016, a plan was made to build a model housing estate following the WUWA example.

Nowe Żerniki – Wrocław's model housing estate

The initiators of the interesting concept of the *Nowe Żerniki* housing estate intended it to be an alternative to the mass, unified, style-deprived housing that was forced by the market. Some of the best Wrocław architects worked on the project. The newly built estate is expected to meet the demands of contemporary residents of Wrocław, enhance social relations, be environmentally friendly and become an architectural icon of Wrocław as the European Capital of Culture 2016. It will be infrastructurally well developed, and the semi-public and public spaces are to be precisely designed. Residential buildings will be diversified in terms of form and ownership. The complex is located in the western part of the outer circle of the city centre, near the AOW ring road and the Municipal Stadium. The construction of this model estate was preceded by sociological research about its architectural shape and social character.

The advertising slogans sounded convincing, as did the idea of a modern housing environment characterised by high-quality architecture. The estate was intended to be visionary, to be built from public sources (financed by the city), to refer to the modernist German WUWA, or even be contemporary Wrocław's answer to it. Yet, as a result of problems with financing this interesting project, the complex ended up as yet another real estate development, albeit a socially oriented one that is supported by a few well-known Wrocław architects. The main real estate developer advertises the newly built habitat as a "model estate" and called it "a Time Spiral", which perhaps is a reference to the history of architecture in Wrocław.

I believe that architecture needs to be supported by the knowledge of potential residents and their social world, including architecture itself, in order to create friendly, safe and highly aesthetic living environments and influence lifestyles. It should be visionary and trendsetting (like in the case of Bauhaus and WUWA, but unfortunately not the wasted opportunity of WUWA2) on a regional and local level. Instead of designing spaces for no one, deprived of identity and cultural values, it should co-create places to live and work in the process of social dialogue. Architecture should be enhanced by reflections about space and its organisation that can be found in the ideas and postulates of new urbanism and that subtly combine tradition with modernity (such as Zbigniew Maćków's project to modernise and develop the interwar department store *Renoma* in Wrocław). This way of designing urban space prevents schematism, formalism and conservatism and preserves historical and cultural continuity, coherence and avant-garde vision in the architectural space of a city.

Conclusions

To conclude, it should be highlighted that there have been discernable changes in the architectural space of Wrocław. Regardless of whether they are critically or positively evaluated by experts or residents, successful or unsuccessful, interfere in the urbanist structure of a historic city or are too timidly modern, they do occur. The major changes are as follows:

- Instead of one ideology that dominates architecture, there is a diversity of ideas and reflections on architecture;
- Instead of ignoring individuals and their needs, architecture is increasingly humanistic, individualistically oriented and creates an identity of a place;
- Instead of distorted modernism and monolithic concrete, postmodernism and diversity of building materials are evident;
- Instead of grey elevations, colour is introduced;
- Instead of factories, there are technology parks and office buildings (characteristically, with *tower* in their name, which exemplifies a trend for English names);
- Instead of shopping streets with welcoming windows, large shopping centres and shopping *galleries* (not selling art) are prevalent, sometimes resembling barracks, which concentrate the commercial function of the city and depopulate the city centre;

- Instead of large housing complexes made of concrete blocks, there are apartment buildings and estates (often gated) or even neighbourhoods of detached houses;
- Instead of cosy, intimate cinemas, there are multiplexes as entertainment centres;
- Aspirations for higher, more prestigious and business-oriented buildings, as exemplified by the controversial skyscraper *Sky Tower*;
- Instead of consistency, there is even greater dispersion and fragmentation;
- Instead of a view of the city's architecture, there are omnipresent advertisements, mostly in a large format;
- Domination of individualised car culture (and a permanent lack of parking space) but also a slow return to collective transport, pedestrian traffic (*city for people*) and integration of the river with the city.

It is worth noting that transformations of the architectural space in Wrocław occur in a city that was rebuilt after World War II (almost 70% was destroyed) according to the socialist ideology, which focused on functionality rather than style, and that was modernised in times of capitalist ideology but still with the emphasis on functionality and thriftiness instead of style and the humanistic values of beauty, moderation and harmony. The way Wrocław urban space is being created and reflected on is dominated by particularism and continues to lack a coherent vision. While in the socialist system architectural vision and creativity were hindered by the authorities, today they are hindered mostly by investors' money and taste.

Space is a product of society at a particular stage of its development. Its nature and quality depends on the culture of its co-creators and their attitude to nature. In the process of social development, every epoch leaves its own layer of products and artefacts. It also leaves nature exploited and destroyed to some extent. Architecture is a product of a society, and its quality and influence on nature depends on the characteristics of this society: its predispositions, attitudes, ideas, values and social institutions in a broad sense of the term. Every period in the social and cultural development of a city generates urban space according to the ideas and values that dominate at the time. These values and ideas unite and penetrate each other, creating a composed, coherent whole. The essence of a city or its genius loci is demonstrated by its multiple layers, the growth of socio-spatial structures depicting the rich culture of the past and a variety of lifestyles, types of housing environments and architectural forms.

These immanent features of cities also refer to Wrocław. Thus, they should be protected and continued. No city, including Wrocław, is a completed formation. Being a product of society and culture, the city is still in the making, it is transforming and developing, combining the past, the present and the future. If societies only followed fashions, trends and current needs, there would not be, for example, any historical monuments because everything old and out of fashion would be seen as clutter. There were periods in the development of European cities when one did not care as much as today about cultural heritage and historical buildings and the question whether to destroy or renovate was not rhetorical. Of course, it is easier to build from scratch than to introduce architectural changes in spaces that are already organised in some way. However, continuity and consistency of architectural space are urbanist cultural values.

The process of development of Polish cities, which is at an earlier stage in comparison to Western Europe, has a chance to learn from the mistakes of others, i.e., to wisely observe Western cities and draw conclusions from their architectural and urban planning successes and failures and to implement wise ideas that take due account of Polish local context and realities. The authorities and architects in Wrocław are increasingly better prepared to create spaces and places thanks to foreign examples as well as their search for authentic, local methods of architectural development of the city.

Katarzyna Kajdanek & Jacek Pluta

Bike Power: Emergence of the Cycling Movement in the Urban Public Sphere

Abstract: In their analysis of Wrocław social movement, the authors of this chapter use Anthony Giddens's theory of reflexivity as well as the conceptual framework of the political process model (McAdam 1982). They demonstrate how in the structuration process (Giddens 2003) an emerging social movement co-creates a new institutional order in the urban public sphere and thus allows actors to develop agency. The analysed social movement is an example of a change that relates to the gradual disappearance of the transformation paradigm.

Keywords: *social vacuum*, new social movement, political process structure, bicycles, Wrocław

The paradox of *social vacuum*

In the late 1970s, in his portrayal of Polish society based on empirical research, one of the leading Polish sociologists of his generation, Stefan Nowak (1979: 160), developed a theory of *sociological* (social) *vacuum* that stretches between the most important spheres of life of many Poles: family and other primary groups based on friendship, and the national community based on ethos. The vacuum in question involved a deficit of *Gesellschaft*-based ties and manifested itself in responses to poll questions. Poles did not express any aspirations (values) related to the public sphere, which, according to Nowak, suggested their social apathy or, at best, withdrawal. Poles demonstrated a conscious lack of civic engagement in public issues that were in their interest and under the control of the authorities. Nowak's theory, repeated in his paper published in *Scientific American* (1981), is one of the most intensely discussed diagnoses of Polish society and, in the eyes of many, remains valid.

There are several reasons for this. The first, quite paradoxically, involved Nowak's diagnosis appearing to be quickly disproven. A year after publication, in 1980, a Carnival of Solidarity[1] started in Poland, followed by the introduction of martial law in December 1981. At the time, a mass social movement symbolised by *Solidarność* [Solidarity], the first trade union that was independent from

---

1   Carnival of Solidarity: a period when the power of the communist regime clearly decreased, e.g. censorship was suspended and the activity of trade unions was allowed.

the communist government, garnered an all-time high of 10,000,000 members and became the subject of Alain Touraine's famous analysis, *The Voice and the Eye* (1981). The discrepancy between the theory of social vacuum and the subsequent course of events, or in fact the inability to predict a social outburst on such a scale, which included many young people, was a blemish on the image of academic sociology. Following these events, attempts were made to explain this weakness from a theoretical perspective (Szawiel 1982). Stimulating a discussion on the validity of Nowak's theory, they also maintained the belief that Poles were unwilling to act on behalf of public issues.

The theory of social vacuum continues to return and provoke intense discussion in relation to the current evaluation of the condition of society. Against the background of generally positive tenor of social and economic transformations in Poland after 1989, a problem that seems to be often highlighted by research is the low level of bonding and bridging social capital, resulting in reluctance to take institutionalised action in the public sphere. A telling example is a small proportion (13%) of adult Poles who are members of non-government organisations, declines in voter turnouts in local and national elections and distrust of public authorities (Sułek 2013). These phenomena seem to demonstrate a generalised reluctance to sustain partner relations between the authorities and citizens, therefore supporting the theory of social vacuum.

In his comment on the results of a panel study entitled *Social diagnosis*, Antoni Sułek (2013: 283–284) states:

> The study [the results of the *Social diagnosis*; authors' note] demonstrates how little social and civil experience Poles have. This experience is gained through activity in organisations, participation in grassroots social initiatives, public meetings or voluntary work. If Poles associate so poorly, if they rarely take action to benefit other people, organisations and their own communities, if they reluctantly gather to decide on something and then do it together, they do not have opportunities to learn organised social action or acquire abilities necessary to live in a civil society. Poles do not know how to organise themselves or act together effectively, unless they go on strike or protest – against constructing a road in the neighbourhood, building a landfill site for the disposal of someone else's waste or a hospice in their town. They do not know how as they have never learnt it from their poor experience. They do not know how because they do not act and they do not act because they do not know how – this is a vicious circle of community action.

Is this true? Is the above quoted diagnosis, supported by the results of comprehensive empirical research based on a large sample of Poles, accurate? Not necessarily. Interpretation of the data that was analysed in this study or in fact a reflection on the data that was not included in it, is crucial. Referring to Alain Touraine's (2013) recent comments, the mistake we make resides in our assumption that society based on the national state has the power to organise public life and to dictate our understanding of the contemporary world. The sociologist's power to judge is decreasing. As Touraine argues, sociologists need a new paradigm to study social change. It is impossible to notice it using traditional sociological tools, mainly because the observation of the traditionally institutionalised public sphere, with its political organisations, is not particularly enlightening, in contrast to the observation of private (non-public) life or culture. By calling a new social subject into life, the contemporary era provides a chance for new knowledge. A new actor appears in the public sphere in place of old organisations: an individual who is endowed with agency and is motivated by an ethical imperative stemming from a sense of dignity, rather than by a desire to maximise profit, which was characteristic of homo economicus. It is therefore important to reinterpret the phenomena that emerge in the public sphere to avoid judgments that do not accurately characterise the specificity of contemporary societies.

Confrontation of the theory of a reproducing *social vacuum* with observable social change is a perfect opportunity to learn more about potential agency-endowing activity in the public sphere. Therefore, in addition to providing theoretical context, this chapter brings the analysis and interpretation to a local level. The subject under consideration is the activity of Wrocław residents associated with an informal urban cycling movement that exemplifies civil engagement. It is, doubtlessly, a vivid example of the aforementioned social change. Rather than focusing on social activity alone, the authors are interested in the fact that forms of activity undertaken by urban movements may, in some respects, confirm reluctance or even aversion to formalising public activity, as demonstrated by the *social vacuum*. Thus, the chapter provides an analysis of new forms of local agency with humbleness and a belief that the discussed cycling movement and the engagement of its members, which exemplify a broader phenomenon of urban movement activity, pose a challenge to contemporary sociological studies.

Social control of historicity in a community – social change and urban movements

The emergence of social movements in Poland is related to changing structural conditions of social order that result in new forms of civil energy. Analysing the nature and source of these transformations, researchers who study social processes explain them by referring to mass consumption accompanied by cultural change (Bauman, Baudrillard), to the information technology revolution (Castells), mobility (Urry) and globalisation (Sassen). Increased reflexivity as a generalised attitude of social actors in late modernity (Giddens) should also be listed as one of the factors.

Global social processes grew in importance in Poland as people born after 1989 came of age. This moment also connects to the gradual fall of the transformation era, which until recently significantly influenced narratives and dominant attitudes in the public sphere. In 1999 Jerzy Buzek's government, the last that descended directly from the Solidarity ethos, simultaneously introduced four important reforms that moulded social order in Poland: a local government and administration reform, a reform of the pension system, a reform of the educational system, and a reform of the medical care system. The vigorous public debate that accompanied them was the last debate with a clearly modernistic tone and it ended with the process of the integration of Poland into Western economic structures. The ultimate symbol of this process was the accession of Poland to the European Union in 2004. Joining the Schengen zone in 2007 was accompanied by gradual opening of the labour market and free movement of goods, services and persons. Poles, particularly the young generation of people born in a free Poland, increasingly often manifest attitudes and expectations similar to those of residents of other nations of the EU. The emergence of new urban movements in Poland fits within a new, post-transformational narrative, which includes an expectation that the Polish public sphere should be more social in the face of modernity.

Theories of social change aim to reveal what is hidden behind these expectations and explain contemporary society by referring to the *agency factor* (Sztompka 2002: 529). This factor emphasises the role of agency in individual and social actions (Giddens, Archer, Sztompka). Agency as a central category in the theory of social becoming (Sztompka 1991) exposes the interrelatedness of individual and structural elements. Agency is neither an attribute of individuals or groups nor a potentiality of social structures. It is a product of the activities of society members and of the structural conditions in which they act. While these conditions provide individuals with resources and possibilities, they also exert pressure and impose restraints. Thus, rather than a state or a quality, agency is a process *in between* action and structure.

Reflexivity is what combines social change and agency. According to Anthony Giddens, "the reflexive monitoring of activity is a chronic feature of everyday action" (1984: 5) and involves the entire social situation: the conduct of the individual, of others and the physical context of the situation. Reflexive monitoring is a complex process and, as Giddens observes, it reveals its hermeneutic nature in two ways. First of all, it involves practical consciousness combined with elements of discursive consciousness that are important to build the motivation to act (1984: 288). In this sense, both practical and discursive consciousness are juxtaposed with the limited influence of the unconscious. In his polemic with Freud, Giddens warns against overestimating the negative influence of unconscious motivations embedded in non-reflexive elements of a personality structure on an individual's ability to control a situation. Secondly, the process of reflexive monitoring has a practical and therefore a social aspect. Being-in-the-world has clear social, material and temporal aspects that constitute a framework for what is experienced and how.

Giddens' hermeneutic interpretation of action is in clear opposition to the Weberian tradition, and directly translates into his understanding of social processes. Importantly, this chapter adopts Giddens' argumentation in the approach to the nature of social change. The authors assume that regular social practices that belong to the sphere of social agency have structural qualities. They influence the rules and borders of institutional order in the sphere of public life, which results from the nature of action and its logical connection with power (Giddens 1984: 14), understood as the capacity to achieve a desired or intended outcome (Ibid.: 15). Power thus becomes a tool of social control. Rather than a manifestation of a social relation, it is an attribute of individual and collective action. "No study of the structural properties of social systems can be successfully carried on, or its results interpreted, without reference to the knowledgeability of the relevant agents" (Giddens 1984: 329).

Social movements, urban movements

Leaving aside details of the debate on theories of social movements that have been comprehensively discussed elsewhere (Diani 1992, Lee 2010), it should be noted that social movement is a kind of agency that is manifested in action and that causes actors in the public sphere to become involved in conflictual relations with a clearly defined opponent on political or cultural grounds. The premise of this argument can be found in Charles Tilly's work (1979), who believed that the essence of social movement lies in the interactions between those who hold power and the representatives of those who are deprived of power, hence the emancipating power of social movements. In groups in the name of which the movements act, conflictual interactions lead to an increase in awareness. They also have an important role in the development of movements' identity as they provide a basis for their legitimation. Through their actions, the members of social movements create networks of informal bonds. They share values and are driven by the sense of solidarity that follows from emancipation. As a general rule, the activity of social movement is critical and consists of publicly expressed demands for change in distribution and exercise of power, and support for these demands in the form of public demonstrations of social support. Due to these characteristics of social movements, Manuel Castells (2013) sees them as an eternal motivating force for social change.

The urban location of social movements and, particularly, making urban space the object of their activity gave rise to a discussion on distinguishing *urban* social movements (Pickvance 2003; Pickvance 1985; Castells 1983; Castells 2013). Therefore, an urban movement can be defined as a kind of territorially rooted social movement that aims to meet the needs of collective consumption, cultural identity and political power in the best possible way (Castells 1983: 342). A stage for these actions is set in the urban public space, which is crucial due to the role it has in big cities. Experts in urban studies emphasise that contemporary cities develop under the domination of consumption processes and the public space of cities adapts its functions to the requirements of the consumer society and is dominated by its logic. As a result, it becomes an organised system of opportunities that serve to satisfy culturally fuelled needs that create an urban lifestyle (Clark 2011). The essence of urban movements lies in the reason they come into conflict with representatives of local government: they manifest a critical attitude towards the identity between the order of the consumer society and the order of urban public space, for which the local government is a political guarantor.

The aforementioned contemporary context is a background for the activity of new social movements in Poland, and has been observable for several years. Not only is this phenomenon accompanied by a whiff of novelty, it also attracts professional interest, the reason for which has already been discussed in this chapter. Referring to the theory of *social vacuum* that was presented earlier, the activity of Polish social movements contradicts the thesis of the reproduction of *social vacuum* in Polish society.

One of these movements, which will be analysed in detail later in this chapter, is a Wrocław urban movement that supports utility cycling. The history of the cycling movement in Wrocław dates back at least 15 years (see *the Calendar of Events*). It comprises frequently undertaken actions and protests that are diverse and, most importantly, long-term, which demonstrates the continuing presence of the movement in the urban public sphere. In a broader context, these activities result from the process of the movement gaining agency and prove its real influence on the organisation of public space. This diagnosis makes one reflect on the form and social consequences of actions that impact the relations between the authorities and the residents in the urban public sphere.

The constitution of the Wrocław cycling movement generally consists of several overlapping processes. First of all, according to what has been already discussed, the agency of the movement is generally linked to how Wrocław residents reflexively monitor events in the urban public space and thus become active participants in it as a result of the hermeneutic moment (Giddens 2003: 339), which is a requirement for breaking routine. The residents' reflexivity means that different forms of knowledge are connected with motivation for action and, consequently, with actions. In this particular case, this knowledge is related to the rules for the creation of transportation policy and its weaknesses and it influences the development of the needs and interests of a movement's members.

As this chapter will demonstrate, reflexivity influences the motivation for action, not only by raising the awareness of one's needs; it also relates to the evaluation of social situations and thus develops the competence that is necessary to act. Effective action requires knowledge of how to mobilise others to gather around shared values, how to act within one's own constraints and the condition of road and transport infrastructure. The cycling movement's direct power depends also on the level of social and cultural competence and capital of its members and their knowledge of urban public space and its resources.

Moreover, development and change in the cycling movement are influenced by wider social and cultural conditions that impact all the participants of the public sphere, including the movement. Bearing this in mind, authors who deal with issues related to social movements (della Porta and Diani 2009) identify four major problem areas in the studies of social movements. They are: relations between cultural changes and transformations of the patterns of social conflict; cultural representations in a social conflict; the process of transforming values and ideas into collective action and, finally, the influence of the transforming forms of agency (related to political, social and cultural changes) on the success or failure of social movements. The following discussion on these four problems serves to outline the background of the emergence of agency and reflexivity in the Wrocław cycling movement.

The anatomy of the Wrocław cycling movement

The choice of words in the above subtitle is not incidental, as urban movements are characterised by a complex structure. Their specificity comprises elements that are typical of contemporary social movements as well as properties that result from a diagnosis of contemporary Polish society. Thus, an accurate portrayal of a cycling movement must combine the evaluations of its key, interrelated components.

- **The essence of the conflict and its socio-cultural background**

Resistance is what constitutes urban movements; conflicts make them visible. In the analysed case of the Wrocław cycling movement, critical diagnosis of urbanity in terms of management of city resources and satisfying residents' needs is an important source of conflict. The essence of this conflict is the creation of cycling rules and guidelines and the development of cycling infrastructure. One party in the conflict is represented by active cyclists and ordinary residents who, using bicycles as a means of transport, enjoy their right to the city. The other party is represented by the municipality. By playing the different interests of diverse users of the public space against each other, the municipality introduces imbalance between the authorities and the residents in the public sphere.

Regardless of the matter under dispute, conflicts primarily reveal the institutional patterns of the local authority's activity in the public sphere, as well as its limitations. The *omnipotence model*, in which the local authority arrogates the right to identify residents' needs and to distribute resources to satisfy them, is losing popularity to the *consumption model* in which the authorities believe that their actions are what the residents desire. While in this model social agents are not reduced to a statistical conversion factor that measures available resources and their needs are important to the authorities, these needs are also subjected to the process of alienation. In a globalised society ruled by mass consumption, the organisation of space is optimised. Thus, the needs of social agents become more important than the agents (i.e., the local community or newcomers: guests or tourists), who become replaceable elements. Needs that are considered important by the authorities are those that contribute to an increase in the attractiveness of a city as a site of consumption.

In contrast, the *reflexive model* that is desired by urban movements presupposes that the local authority has a limited capability to recognise the needs of residents. The only effective method to satisfy those needs is to refer to the residents' ability to co-create urban policy. To provide objective conditions that improve the quality of urban life, the representatives of city dwellers and the local authority become partners in organising the city space. Thus, in the case of urban mobility policy, the authorities' role is neither to decide arbitrarily how Wrocław's residents should move around the city nor to design transportation ideas according to what they believe people expect. As urban movements underline, it is necessary to incorporate residents of the city into the processes of co-creating the mobility policy in terms of legal regulations, infrastructure planning and the promotion of individual mobility in order to counter-balance the negative effects of long-term prioritisation of car traffic.

The discussed conflict has a double nature: it is political because it concerns a change in the mode of governing a city and it is cultural because it refers to values and norms that underlie the decisions that are made. Different visions of social order, which are sources of this conflict, indisputably exist. However, it is unclear why the question of social order is becoming the driving force of change. In order to understand it, one needs to refer to the national policy and to a broader social context of changes that combines Polish specificity with more general qualities of modernity.

As for the Polish context, the most important source of change is the gradual exhaustion of public narrative about the need for political transition and public values, such as the market economy and the middle class (Ziółkowski 1999; Wnuk-Lipiński and Ziółkowski 2001; Jarosz 2008; Krzemiński 2010). The erosion of these values in Poland proceeds together with the consolidation of institutions that are characteristic of developed democracies and economies operating in a globalised world. Polish accession to most of the important European and Atlantic structures has contributed to this phenomenon. However, paradoxically, the gradual foundation of public order, which was a socially shared Polish dream at the beginning of the 1990s, undermined the aspirations of the authorities and decreased the quality of politics. The possibility or even desirability of building a civil society is gradually disappearing. The demand for creating a middle class as a desired element of social structure is now empty words (Domański 2002). Are there Polish politicians that even use the term? Instead, the current public debate has become critical of public institutions and their operating rules (Wróblewski and Dobroszek 2014).

This criticism, however, is not homogenous and its sources are diverse. While on a national level there is an increase in conservative moods and the political scene is moving to the right, on a local level the situation is different. The new public narrative that is used by social movements clearly refers to contemporary problems and has a generational character. People born after 1989 come to the fore, and their most reflexive fraction is the "angry precariat" (Standing 2011). New elements are introduced in place of the old, outdated narrative. They are connected with the radicalisation of political aims, transformation of public values and exchange of political elites who are partly "worn out". The results of local elections in major Polish cities (Wrocław, Warsaw, Cracow) in 2014 symbolically confirmed this change. The support for the city mayors who had been in office for many years was far below their expectations, while the candidates who either knew how to incorporate social movements and their aims into the agenda (Hanna Zdanowska in Łódź) or who previously were members of urban movements (Jacek Jaśkowiak in Poznań) won. Jarosław Makowski, head of the Civic Institute – a think tank of the Civic Platform political party – said in an interview:

Does the narrative about Poland as a country under construction speak to Poles? No, it does not! The local elections have demonstrated it. The accents have shifted. Quality of life is crucial, rather than building from concrete and steel. Poles want to live comfortably and it is not surprising. Quality of life is important for the middle class, which has not been yet created in Poland. It is bad, because in Western Europe, but here as well, middle class is a condition of social stability.[2]

Although on a local level there are voices that urban movements have little potential for stimulating social change (Lenkowski 2014; Borejza 2015), change is undoubtedly occurring and it has an institutional character. Interestingly, this transformation takes place within the *social vacuum*. In other words, the increase in interest in the local public sphere is not accompanied by the process of filling the *social vacuum* with social activities in traditional forms, such as political parties or non-governmental institutions. In their activity, urban activists usually use resources of the public sphere that are typical of contemporary society, in which individuals in informal networks play the leading role.

- ## The role of informal networks

Dense informal social networks distinguish social movements from other collective actions. These networks are developed in the process of interaction between individuals as a result of long-term participation in the exchange of resources for the achievement of a common goal, while the individuals retain their autonomy and independence. The internet has become the primary medium for creating networks. The use of mobile devices and social networking applications was a turning point in the process of forming new social movements. Traditional forms of association declined in importance, while it became crucial to draw the interest of the media (and other audiences) into subjects that are significant for social movements. Aside from generating media interest, new applications allow members and supporters to communicate, disseminate their ideas or even gather funds. Manuel Castells (2013) observed many *Twitter revolutions,* i.e. the forms of civil mobilisation that took place simultaneously in urban public space and the autonomous internet space. In his opinion, mass individualised communication (Castells 2013, 2010) was the source of development of the network society, i.e. the background against which social movements of the 21st century operate.

The popularity of the new media provoked a debate about the *click-activism* phenomenon, i.e. a superficial form of engagement in social movements

---

2   http://www.polskatimes.pl/artykul/3682608,makowski-w-polsce-nastepuje-odrodzenie-mieszczanstwa-jego-symbolem-sa-ruchy-miejskie,2,id,t,sa.html

by clicking the *like* button on social networking websites. Researchers of this phenomenon have convincingly demonstrated the ephemerality of Facebook-mediated engagement in their analysis of the "Save Darfour" case (Lewis et al. 2014; compare Andrzejewski 2014). They point at the urgent need to develop a strategy of using new media in civil society so that mediated civil engagement has a deeper and more durable character (Nugroho and Syarief 2012). In the face of the difficulties in management and effective use of online activism, it is advisable to combine new technologies with offline grassroots activities.

In the analysed Wrocław cycling movement, there are informal networks of contacts and exchanges of resources that constitute human capital (knowledge, skills) and social capital (trust, cooperation). Sharing resources during important events is particularly significant. The monthly Critical Mass, the annual cycling festival, free bike repair events, bike breakfasts and teas and other projects that are considered to be elements of the same protest build solidarity and maintain a sense of belonging even after the initiatives are over.

Social networking services (Facebook), in which cycling movements are very active, also play a significant role. The second edition of participatory budgeting in Wrocław (2014) was an example of the use of new media and social networking to mobilise residents around the aims of the cycling movement. While the turnout for the first edition was only 40,000 (6.25% of the city population), almost 160,000 residents (25%) voted in the second edition, of whom 10% voted on a citywide project to build 10 kilometres of bicycle paths as part of a proposal developed by activists from the cycling movement. Most of the promotional campaign of the project (and of the participatory budgeting) was run with the use of a website and a Facebook event. As a result, almost 2/3 of the votes on the project were cast online and 1/3 on ballot papers collected in person.

Building contact networks and actions taken by reflexive individuals with high levels of social and cultural competence are increasingly common, which results in permanent demand for change of the institutional order. Urban movements, using practical knowledge (how to act) and discursive knowledge that analyses the conditions for action, have an impact on the functioning of the urban public sphere. A clear example is the change in the way in which local authorities speak about urban policy. It is hard to find a mayor of a big Polish city who does not include at least part of the postulates of urban movements regarding improving the quality of life in a city (e.g. introduction of participatory budgeting, building cycle paths or playgrounds) into his or her political agenda. It cannot be ruled out, however, that this openness to the needs of residents may only be a part of the election campaign.

In order to exert influence independently from the election calendar, urban movements seek methods to make changes in rhetoric be followed by changes in practice. These efforts are observed by the supporters of urban movements, but even more closely by their opponents. More radical groups criticise urban movements for exerting weak pressure and little efficiency in putting postulates into practice, as a result of the use of improper tools and excessive focus on the identity of the movement instead of solving problems. As the representatives of a Warsaw squat *Syrena* wrote (Wierszot and Kocinia 2015): "Urban movements cannot provide an alternative while they are trapped within the framework of civil society. To make a change, they would need to abandon their professional activism, commit class suicide and share their tools and connections for the sake of direct actions aimed at transformation of the relations of power".

This diagnosis poses a problem of authenticity for the identity of urban movements. On the one hand, to be active members, individuals need to cross the boundaries of their social world, framed by their professional roles or social position, and establish their new identities. On the other hand, urban movements face a problem of their own institutional identity. In its traditional, associative form, it is counter-productive for the continuance of the movement. This problem is becoming increasingly significant for urban movements.

Collective identity

To be permanent, an institutional change of social order must meet certain structural conditions. Urban movement that legitimises such a change faces the necessity of defining its **collective identity**, i.e., the recognition and development of a sense of community shared by individuals who are involved in collective action. This sense of community is based on a realisation of the common goal and recurrent participation in various activities, which, put together, build a sense of belonging to a social movement. Finding social support is another important, although not prioritised, element of building a collective identity. What urban movements want becomes less important than who creates them and who represents them.

Depicting the context of the development of urban movements in Poland, Paweł Kubicki suggests that urban movements should be recognised as cultural movements rather than social movements. This is due to the specificity of Polish society, being alienated from urbanity and formed by the nobility and peasants rather than the bourgeoisie. New bourgeoisie – i.e., generations that were raised in cities that lack urban traditions but aspire to them – are forced to search for elements of urbanity that are later incorporated into their identity structure. The value that underlies behavioural norms of the new bourgeoisie is the city defined as a common good rather than a sum of private properties that was a characteristic of the nobility-peasantry model. As a result of the process of searching for urban values in rediscovered cities, the developing urban movements aim to socialise the public sphere. Taking advantage of the urban boom (Kubicki 2009), they also try to encourage other residents to share their ideas.

The values and aims of urban movements (urbanity and a high quality of life) seem to represent the worldview of the new bourgeoisie. However, the postulates of urban movements do not specify who the addressees of these postulates are, which is particularly clear in the case of the postulate on the right to the city (Harvey 2012; Majer 2010; Lefebvre 2012) that is often attached to urban movements. There are two ways of understanding the right to the city today. The first is genetically leftist and conflict-based; the other is not aligned with the Marxist tradition but results from a process of formation of an urban citizen who has never before formed any expectations towards the city (Pluciński 2013).

Critics of urban movements believe that including the right to the city (in the former understanding of the term) in the agenda of urban movements is irrational because the essence of the problem is low social competence for exercising the right to the city, rather than the need to provide this right (as the system of direct democracy provides it, see Lenkowski 2014). What is more, according to the critics, although the right to the city (according to the latter definition) sounds like a universal slogan, it in fact covers particular interests of well-organised and efficient lobby groups and it has little in common with the idea of the right to the city for all citizens. As one of the authors notes:

> One of the popular postulates that hide behind the right to the city is making cities more bicycle-friendly (building cycle paths, etc.). I do not see anything bad about this postulate. I would like the cycling infrastructure in my city resemble Rotterdam more than… Tbilisi. However, it is hypocritical to hide this postulate, which is beneficial mostly for the young (or those in the prime of their life) and healthy people who use bicycles, behind the universal slogan of the right to the city. Why should bicycle infrastructure be developed under this slogan?[3]

There is also another problem, related to the fact that Harvey's words about a right to the city involves class structure. Urbanisation is a class process in which those who own the means of production (elites) exert an influence on urban landscape that is consistent with their interests. This situation can only be changed by political self-organisation and demonstration of social activity (Harvey 2012). However, as Kubicki suggests, changes in Polish cities are cultural rather than class-related. The proletariat (or precariat) do not use the slogan of the right to the city. Those

---

3   Lenkowski Błażej http://www.instytutobywatelski.pl/22225/lupa-instytutu/ruchy-miejskie-spojrzenie-z-dystansu, accessed 6 July, 2015.

who do are educated, left-oriented citizens who reject an urban policy that follows the rules of global capitalism. The new bourgeoisie realise that as a consequence of the logic of neoliberal development that was adopted by local authorities, cities lose their agency and the new bourgeois lose the city, i.e., the common good that underlies their identity. The concern for city and urbanity is greater in the Polish cities where the urban tradition is relatively short and weak and "Polish decision-makers continue to use mental categories that derive from the tradition of nobility vs. peasantry, defining city as a conglomerate of private properties" (Kubicki 2012).

Today, these two different cultural models collide in the space of Polish urban areas and determine the specificity of the urban rebellion expressed by Polish urban movements.

The urban cycling movement – political and cultural factors

While so far this chapter has focused on the origin and specificity of Polish urban movements, referring mainly to macrostructural qualities of the social order, this section will mostly examine the logic of action of urban movements and the evaluation of their social consequences. The political process model (Tilly 1978; McAdam 2008; compare Kolasa-Nowak 1999) is particularly useful in the analysis of the conditions of action of urban movements and their impact on social change. The elements of this model include the political opportunity structure, indigenous organisational strength and a sense of cognitive liberation.

The political opportunity structure is a term that describes factors external to the movement, particularly the open or closed nature of the political system. As McAdam (2008: 21–27) notes, the political opportunity structure is rarely resistant to change, and broad social processes (modernisation, industrialisation, globalisation), as well any intervention, particularly of urban movements, loosens the structure and contributes to undermining the social system. The level of susceptibility to change is also indicated by the stability of the electorate, the presence of powerful allies, and, finally, the degree of tolerance towards change among the elite.

Another important component of the political process model is the *organisational readiness* of the members of a social movement, i.e. the indigenous potential to convert a favourable structure of political opportunities into an organised campaign of social protest. Contact between members is crucial to organising efficiently, as are the ensuing *solidary incentives*, i.e. interpersonal rewards that provide motivation for participation in the movement. The more efficient the communication inside and outside the movement, the greater the opportunity for interaction (Castells 2013; Van Aelst and Walgraave 2004: 12). The organisational readiness is also determined by leaders of the movement, in particular by their organisational and political skills and charisma.

The third element of the model is *insurgent consciousness*, i.e. a collective evaluation of the opportunity to protest that is formed by collective definition of the situation, sensitivity to signals from the elite and from allies and the collective response to these signals. Only with collective recognition that protest is necessary and has a chance of success can this protest take place.

• The past, the present and the future

Social movements have an evolutionary character; people who are involved in activities related to it give it diverse organisational forms and different images. Movements emerge, and seemingly die down to then appear in a new form, with new slogans that express similar ideas. Following Pluciński (2013), who adopted a double interpretation of the right to the city by distinguishing its leftist and pragmatic origin, one may say that at its beginnings, in the 1990s, the essence of the left-oriented cycling movement was political conflict and rebellion. However, both the movement and the idea of the right to the city evolved. As today the postulates of the cycling movement meet favourable conditions, the movement can establish goals that neither come into conflict with other ideologies nor are in contradiction with involvement in the activities of the local authorities (the so-called hacking of the system).

Figure 1: The map of the network of cycle tracks and paths in Wrocław in 2009 and 2013

Source: http://gis.um.wroc.pl/imap/

In the 1990s in Wrocław, there was one cycling organisation that worked as an open coalition – The Wrocław Cycling Coalition (Polish: Koalicja Rowerowy Wrocław) that derived from environmental organisations. Defining their objectives, the activists wrote in the 1990s: "It is our goal to make the residents of Wrocław drive less and cycle more. Rather than just on Sundays along the Odra river, to encourage people to cycle on an everyday basis: to work, to school, to shops…"[4] The movement rejected the rules of direct democracy and single electoral actions in favour of lobbying (during the Cycling Round Table meetings) and education (outdoor events and giving opinions on projects). The participants noted that a change to the current transport situation in the city would require a strong lobby that cared about the interests of cyclists (and not those of all the residents).

As a result of internal conflicts, the first cycling coalition collapsed in 2006. The Wrocław Cycling Initiative (Polish: Wrocławska Inicjatywa Rowerowa, abbreviated WIR), which was created in its place, adopted most of the goals and working methods of the Coalition. A careful reader of the description of the WIR's goals, however, would notice significant differences between this organisation and the coalition. New elements were added to the range of activities of the movement, i.e. promotional and educational activity related to travel behaviour, focussed on raising social awareness on the subject. Therefore, although indirectly, WIR managed to expand the circle of potential beneficiaries of its activities, extending it to all road users – in broader terms, the entire urban population – even if the interests of cyclists were the priority.

In coordination with the City for Bikes network, WIR members influenced local and national authorities so efficiently that they enjoyed remarkable successes in the field of legal regulations beneficial to cyclists (see *milestones* listed in the *Calendar of Events*). Nonetheless, achievements in this field have not resulted in an increase in the number of regular urban cyclists. Cycling was neither comfortable (lack of cycle paths in the city centre) nor fashionable. There were not many cyclists, particularly those who would present an aspirational image. The time of following German and Dutch patterns of urban cycling was yet to come.

---

4   http://rowery.eko.org.pl/indexoldbike.php?site=o_nas, accessed 6 July, 2015.

Figure 2: The dynamics of the increase in bicycle paths in Wrocław

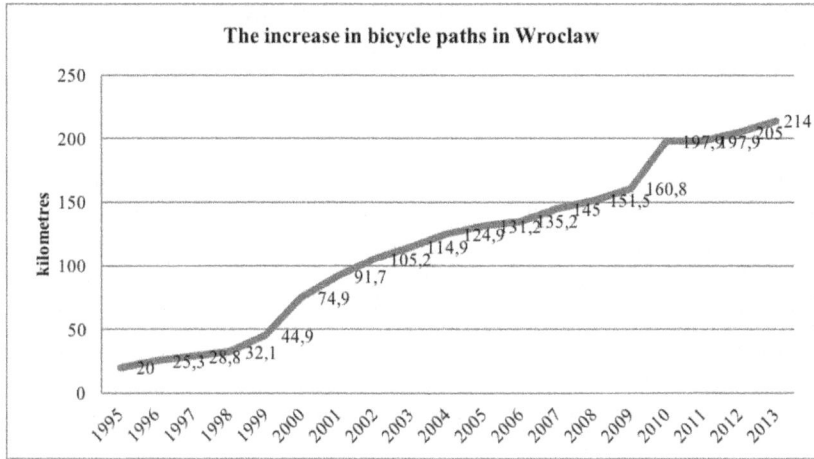

The increase in bicycle paths in Wroclaw

Source: own analysis on the basis of www.wrower.pl

It should be noted that WIR undertook its most spectacular actions when the dominating investing model concentrated on large road construction projects, motorways and development of traffic. This tendency was typical of the transitional period of catching up with Western Europe. Bicycles were mostly associated with recreation or a means of transport for the poor and urban cycling in all weathers was met with mocking smiles. According to the activists at the time (Lubaczewska 2011) the problem lay in the unexploited potential of cooperation between local authorities and non-governmental organisations that popularise cycling. An organisation that would be responsible for soft activities, such as promotion of cycling, sustainable transport, safe travel behaviour, etc., which would be a subsidiary of the local government, was expected to guarantee success. However, there was no such organisation.

The Action City Association (Polish: Akcja Miasto) – the newest actor on the scene of urban cycling movements in Wrocław – was registered in autumn 2014. Many people who constitute Action City today met for the first time on the occasion of promoting a large cycling project proposal that applied for funding in participatory budgeting in Wrocław. Although the main supporters of the idea of making the proposal more social and leaving it in the hands of the citizens had earlier cooperated with WIR, the cooperation could not be continued as a result of incompatibility in visions and goals. WIR sees the source of success mainly in precise methods of exerting pressure on the authorities and lobbying for their interests. The leaders of the emerging Action City believed, on the other hand, that political efficiency involves incorporating as many city residents as possible into the promotion of the project, including the cycling movement. The leaders planned to use social networking sites and to cooperate with other media to convey their main message, i.e., to encourage citizens to exchange cars for bikes and, as a result, make cycling fashionable. After a spectacular success in participatory budgeting, the people involved in the project (which gathered almost 16,000 votes – 10% of the total) felt that they managed to impress the citizens and the authorities, that they were a force that could not be ignored once structured and formalised. During internal discussions, members of the organisation indicated that city and urbanity are their main values and cycling is an element of implementing their vision of a good city to live in.

- **Opportunity structure – creating political context for a cycling movement in a city**

Governmental policy papers are an important factor that influenced the political context of the emergence of the cycling movement. They set goals and directions for change in the methods of exercising power and they provide urban movements with grounds to demand permanent improvements to the political system and better legal regulations on a local level. One of the most important policy papers that influenced thinking regarding the future of Polish cities is the National Urban Policy (Polish: Krajowa Polityka Miejska, abbreviated KPM). The obligation to elaborate on it resulted from an amendment to the act on the development policy regulations that introduced the KPM as a policy paper. The main goal of the KPM is to "strengthen the capacity of cities and urban areas for sustainable development and to create jobs and improve the quality of life of citizens" (KPM 2014:16). The primary objective of the transportation policy (for the years 2006–2025),[5] which is currently under development, is a significant improvement in the quality of the transportation system and its expansion according to the principles of sustainable development as well balance between social, economic and spatial aspects and environmental protection. This set of priorities concerning transportation policy clearly demonstrates the necessity to gradually replace individual car transport with collective public transport and cycling.

Present in official governmental documents but ignored by local authorities, Polish bicycle policy is actually implemented by grassroots movements. There

---

5   The National Transportation Policy: 2006–2025; Polish: Polityka Transportowa
     Państwa na lata 2006–2025.

are active organisations in all major Polish cities that represent everyday users of bicycles and they de facto influence the urban bicycle policy. As their postulates often precede changes, it would be hard to find a pro-cycling initiative that was not first postulated by the community of bikers and then, with greater or lesser resistance, adopted by the local government.

Since the 1990s, a movement focused on social control of the transportation policy has been developing in Poland. Bicycle organisations that are linked in the Cities for Bicycles network function in almost every major Polish city and become visible during Critical Mass events. Since May 2008, a parliamentary group for bicycle transportation and tourism has been in operation. It originated as a result of cooperation between Members of Parliament and cycling organisations. Since July 2008, in the Ministry of Infrastructure, a working group has been adapting Polish legal regulations on bicycles to the EU standards and the requirements of international law. There are also exemplary cases of cooperation between NGOs and local authorities in giving an opinion on infrastructure and policy papers, which demonstrates the relative openness of local governments to social participation in creating bicycle policies and confirms the positive outcome of this participation.

Until quite recently, the participation of Wrocław cycling movements in creating bicycle policy mostly had an informal character, and thus was inefficient. Discussion, public criticism and informal cooperation were the dominating forms of social participation. In recent years, however, cooperation in developing bicycle policy has become structured and the first cooperation in evaluation and programming of bicycle policy has begun.

These changes can be directly linked to the results of local government elections in 2014 when the electorate that was expected to remain stable shook the political scene, which resulted in a second round of voting. The cycling movement used social dissatisfaction with the current redistribution of resources to form expectations about the quality of life of all residents of the city. As a result, the Presidential Bicycle Policy Council was created, which was composed of the representatives of new cycling movements (Action City). On a tide of dissatisfaction, radical factions of urban movements used the mechanism of direct democracy – a referendum – and proposed a question about prioritising the construction of bicycle paths in the city (the proposal was rejected in the end).

The current potential of political opportunity structure is constantly increasing, which is demonstrated by the presence of influential allies of the Wrocław cycling movement. They mostly include cycling movements in other cities as well as the local governments of these cities – Gdańsk, Gdynia, Lublin, Cracow – that use their efforts to support the cycling movement as an element of gaining a competitive advantage over others.

Table 1: Bicycle infrastructure in selected Polish cities in 2017

City	Wrocław	Cracow	Poznań	Gdańsk*	Gdynia*	Sopot	Szczecin	Lublin	Warszawa
Population	634,000	762,000	546,000	461,500	247,800		407,200	341,700	1.7 million
Number of docking stations	76	150	89	No docking stations	-	8	34	90	331
Number of bikes in the system	760	1500	933	3500	-	80	348	891	4869
Length of bicycle paths [in km]	214	165	129	185	70,4	20	98	110	495

*planned for 2018 (for Gdańsk and Gdynia)
Source: own analysis based on wrower.pl, nextbike.pl, GUS.

Finally, it is important to note the increasing tolerance of power elites towards the process of popularisation of cycling. The level of this tolerance varies, of course – different representatives of the authorities, different departments of the city council, different categories of opinion leaders support the ideas of the cycling movement to different extents. Nonetheless, the friendly atmosphere at the meetings of Action City representatives with the President, the development of the Presidential Bicycle Policy Council (of which representatives of the cycling movement are members) and the promotion and wider scope of action and responsibility of the Bicycle Officer demonstrate that increasing participation by the pro-cycling movement in creating urban policy is tolerated more than it was in the past.

- **Modern dilemmas: Creating cultural context for the urban cycling movement**

General analyses by authors like Glen Norcliffe (2001) or Dave Horton (2007) demonstrate that bicycles and cycling can be seen as a medium and a product of modernity. On the other hand, bicycles and cycling can also be perceived as something outdated that should be exchanged for a means of transport that better presents the spirit of increased mobility and wealth, which is observed in the practices of owning and driving cars (Sheller, Urry 2000). It is clear, however, that in many modern and wealthy societies there is a turn towards bicycles, which may be explained as a form of resistance against car culture, which is seen as a symbol of false modernity. As a result, bicycles lose the label of a means of transport for the poor (those who cannot afford a car) and become perceived as an efficient, egalitarian, sustainable form of urban transport (Dubey 2006).

The change of the mobility model in Poland, i.e. replacing cars with other forms of transport, is difficult and it may be interpreted as an element of adjusting to the conditions of late modernity. An important element of this change is the stigma of political transition that is related to Polish consumer attitudes. One of the first effects of the introduction of a free market economy was that households imme- diately started purchasing durable consumer goods. After years of the shortage economy, the shocking picture of full shelves, irrespective of the prices, allowed many Poles to realise their aspirations and dreams related to material symbols of lifestyle interpreted as a liberation from the communist stigma of crisis and poverty and as a form of imitating the stereotypical version of a Western life- style. More than just the first impulse, this process has been continuing despite periodical slowdown in economic growth (Czapiński 2013). It is observable in the dynamics of retail sales growth, which involves mostly non-food goods. Sales growth for food and soft drinks was at 40%, but for non-food goods it was as much as 111% in 2013 (GUS 2014: 75).

The structure of consumption remains important. Passenger cars have a signifi- cant stature among purchased durable goods. In the eyes of Poles, cars, particu- larly of Western brands, are more than a means of transport. They carry symbolic messages expressing the social status of their owners (Szlendak 2010). A car allows its owner to symbolically support values such as privacy or individualism. In the process of fulfilling needs, a lack of spatial limitation is an important component of consumer patterns that express lifestyle and constitute social differences. The opening of Poland to the West simply facilitated this process. Aside from the purchase of new cars by Poles, mass individual importation of second hand cars from Western Europe has been continuing since 1990. As a result, according to the Central Register of Vehicles and Drivers, the average age of a car in Poland is 16 years. According to the recently published statistics by the Central Statistical Office (Polish: Główny Urząd Statystyczny; GUS), the percentage of households that own a passenger car increased from 38% in 1995 to 58% in 2013. In index basis, per 1,000 people there were 120 registered passenger cars in 1989, 320 in 2005 and 500 in 2013 (GUS 2015: 74).

Although the value of luxury goods as symbols of prosperity is depreciating with their increasing accessibility, "such symbols of success in life as (…) owner- ship of a house in a wealthy neighbourhood and a new car" determine belonging to the middle class (Domański 2012: 93). This seemingly unstoppable march of stereotypical modernity in fact encounters barriers to development. These barriers are easy to notice, particularly in cities where the car ownership rate per 1000 residents exceeds the values observed in major European cities. According to the Eurostat data, this coefficient was 530.

A report by the Supreme Audit Office (Polish: Najwyższa Izba Kontroli) from 2010 (2010: 14) that stated the car ownership rate in major Polish cities provoked a vigorous reaction from the general public. In 2009 it was as much as 1189 cars per 1000 people in Warsaw, 642 in Wrocław, 564 in Cracow and 638 in Poznań. What is more, based on policy paper analysis, the report indicated that among 10 major Polish cities, only in Cracow was there a significant increase in the number of people using public transport.

Supporters of removing cars from urban space and promoting other forms of mobility acknowledge that alternative methods of transportation need to compete with the car and try to replace it whenever possible, offering the same comfort (flexibility, convenience, short travel time), because ousting cars from cities is (for now?) impossible (Krysiński 2014: 43). Other researchers (Denis and Urry 2009) even suggest that although the car era is ending because the resources necessary for maintaining car dominance are running low, it is not clear which means of transport could replace the car – i.e., eliminate the negative effects related to car use but be able to maintain the social and economic order that is today supported by the culture of automobility.

If revolution is not possible, an alternative is an evolution that consists of two elements. One of them is an attempt to exert pressure on decision-makers by spreading the message that their decisions create cities based on car traffic, the negative consequences of which are well known. Another significant element of the evolution – the campaign for moving passengers from cars into other means of transport – is the recognition of drivers' motivations and reasons for owning a car followed by an attempt to influence their cognitive and emotional structures and, consequently, an attempt to change transportation patterns. What is more, this influence must be tailored to different categories of passengers and the segmentation should be based on taste as a factor drawing distinctions between social classes (Bourdieu 2005; see Domański 2012: 19).

The problem of class differences in using bicycles has been analysed by Krzysztof Świrek (2012). The dominant class has the power to set patterns of behaviour and define appropriate aesthetic choices – it creates and plays, while the middle class follows and searches for rules of behaviour that would secure their social position. While the working class acknowledges the patterns of other classes, it is anchored in a world that is matched to their competences. What the dominant class values in cycling is the feeling of being close to the city; the warmth of the sun and the caress of the breeze on their face. The dominant class distances itself from bicycles as material objects and instead highlights the independence and freedom that comes with cycling. The middle class uses the bicycle as a symbol of prestige. Therefore, the brand and quality of equipment are considered very important. The main purpose of having a bicycle, i.e. the pleasure of cycling, is overshadowed by seemingly secondary activities – gathering equipment and gadgets and fearing theft because a loss of material goods is also a significant loss for budget and prestige. The working class, which is focused on practical aspects of action, the propensity to save and the instrumental efficiency of practices, treats cycling as an ordinary activity and a bicycle as a *normal* object, which can unite rather than divide people.

It is also interesting how individual experiences of cycling are intercepted and incorporated into dominating political discourses. In other words, it is increasingly difficult just to cycle. The act of cycling is expected to express lifestyle, concern for one's own health and the health of society as a whole, the concern for urban space, etc.

As it irresistibly evolved during the political transition, modern Polish society increasingly often revealed its contradictory character. On the one hand, following other European countries, cultural patterns of late modernity are gradually introduced with cycling as their symbol. On the other hand, the promotion of the bicycle encounters resistance from the ruling elite and social groups who do not acknowledge the synonymy of bicycles and modernity. Contemporary hostility towards the cycling movement can be related to frequent practices of associating cyclists with obsessed environmentalists who want to make everybody else cycle, which is unacceptable for those who see modernity as building motorways.

Only with the passage of time is it possible to see the differences in the processes of the cycling movement's efforts to frame cycling as something that benefits the entire community. Earlier movements (WIR) focused on cycling as a form of struggle against environmental problems, the main beneficiaries of which were the city, the urban community or society as a whole. Selected methods (Critical Mass, criticism of road investments for not including cycling infrastructure) encountered resistance among those who supported modernity based on car culture – mostly the emerging middle class.

Younger movements, such as Action City, highlight urban lifestyle, activity in the public sphere and strengthening local identity and commitment to the city as major benefits of cycling. Individuals and their identities are the main beneficiaries, followed by city dwellers and the city space. Action City creates an image of a city resident: a new bourgeois for whom love of the city is an element of self-identity. This love can be expressed, strengthened and, importantly, spread to others by riding a bike. The environmental profit is important but mostly in the local context, as well as the economic profit that is significant in terms of supporting the local economy.

- **Organisational readiness: creating social context for the urban cycling movement**

In this section, the chapter will return to the problem of Poles' passivity in the public sphere, i.e. their lack of participation in associative forms of action, which was defined as *social vacuum*. Is the activity of social movements becoming a chance to overcome this problem? As studies of local civil engagements demonstrate, 13.7% of Poles belong to organisations, associations, parties, circles etc., and three-quarters of the members are active. Data from 2013 indicates a one percent decrease in comparison to 2011 (Czapiński 2014). The proportion of people who are members of associations increases with the size of the place of residence – it is a little bigger in major cities than in the countryside. On the other hand, the relatively low civil engagement in general public issues is accompanied by a significant increase in the interest in urbanity and the city as objects of reflection and action of many actors in the urban scene.

There is a question, however, as to what extent active urban movements are able to mobilise other residents and city users to articulate their interests and support the movement's actions. An analysis conducted on the basis of a representative study (Kajdanek and Pluta 2016) that aimed to evaluate the potential of Wrocław residents to get involved in the participation process demonstrated that the attitude that "the authorities know better" when it comes to ruling a city remains dominant.

This chapter will now analyse action frames of the urban cycling movement in Wrocław, bearing in mind that a condition of success of an urban movement is formulating the values that underlie the movement so that they reach a wide range of recipients and have mobilising power. Frames are interpretative schemata that allow individuals to place and perceive objects, persons and events from their life in a broader context by simplifying and condensing "the world out there" (Mooney and Hunt 1996).

A first stage of efficient mobilisation of people around the values of the cycling movement is to make them acknowledge that traffic jams, polluted air, erosion of public space, urban sprawl, etc. are social problems resulting from unsustainable development. However, referring to environmental slogans is inefficient. As the results of a study from Copenhagen demonstrate, environmental motivation is only important for 1% of cyclists. According to a survey on the Polish population, only every fifth Pole considers environmental problems a cause for concern. It is interesting that local environmental issues related to one's neighbourhood are considered less threatening than national and global environmental problems (CBOS 2014). Poles seem to think that while environmental threats exist, they endanger someone else somewhere else.

The limited efficiency of introducing change into the social context by the cycling movement in the 1990s resulted partly from their use of environmental arguments in attempts to become a legitimate party in the participation process. These arguments did not resonate with Polish society. The process of legitimisation of the cycling movement as a party in the participation process remains difficult because local administration endeavours to preserve control over management and planning of urban traffic and impose their interpretation of problems rather than include the voice of the cycling movement. A new actor, Action City, justifies its rights with the great social support it received in the vote on participatory budgeting, the rapid institutionalisation of the movement, its recognised role as an accepted commentator on events in the city, good relations with the President and the participation of its members in the Wrocław Social Advisory Council (Polish: Rady społeczne).

From the perspective of interpretative frames, early cycling movements did not refer to the cultural identity of new city citizens as important beneficiaries of their activities (Castells 1983). Instead, they emphasised their focus on the city (and equated urban space with urban community), their efforts to improve the quality of collective consumption, particularly bicycle transport, and their political engagement. The newly formed urban movement – Action City – devotes significantly more space in their interpretative framework to the cultural identity of the new bourgeois. One of Action City's priorities is urbanity and making the city a better place to live by increasing the participation of residents in the process of resource distribution (the participation rule). Like their predecessors, Action City does not specifically refer to social categories of their potential recipients or supporters. Although to some extent politically engaged (i.e. striving for political change in a city using institutional methods), the majority of Action City members prioritise actions manifesting their attachment to the city and to bicycles as identity-building elements, and to the activities focused on strengthening ties and solidarity within the organisation, rather than their political activity. The focus on developing commitment to the city and a modern, urban identity rather than on environmental issues may result in a greater chance to mobilise people around the objectives of the cycling movement than in earlier phases of its activity.

The next step for effective mobilisation is to find methods of implementing changes, determine social configurations that will help to implement them and reach consensus between the movement and its opponents. Under current conditions, there is a clear clash between what is already conceivable by the cycling movement's representatives, and what continues to be inconceivable by their opponents. An interesting recent example of this clash is the discussion about a temporary diversion of one of the most frequented routes in Wrocław city centre, which is more convenient for bicycles than for cars. Observers of the WIR profile on Facebook accused the cyclists of being too ostentatiously happy (a large number of *likes* of the Facebook post) with the convenience designed by the local authorities:

> Your frantic satisfaction with every obstruction of car traffic proves, as always, that you do not want coexistence with others and improvement of your situation but instead to form an exclusive clique and abuse anyone who dares to drive. (…) You can replace all the roads with cycle paths, but success would actually be finding a compromise for everyone, wouldn't it?[6]

Another example of the inconceivable that eventually permeates into social imagination is the annual Wrocław Cycling Festival organised by WIR, which has been recently preceded by promotional campaigns (distributing snacks and beverages sponsored by local restaurants). This year, several thousand cyclists gathered for the event, the city president opened the cycling route and the vice-president responsible for city transport cycled with his family together with the residents. Over the following days, local newspapers wrote about *bike power* and, in his blog, President Dutkiewicz expressed hope that cycling would be a part of the celebration of the European Capital of Culture 2016.

WIR observed quite a long time ago that although the model of social participation in creating cycling policy in Wrocław was relatively advanced and effective, the main weakness of the system was the influence of media campaigns involving cyclists on political activities. Even though the city council has an efficient channel for gathering civil interventions from monitoring social infrastructure, media campaigns often impacted the decision-making process. It seems, however,

---

6   An excerpt from a post on the WIR Facebook fan page (Rowerowy Wrocław) informing that a more convenient diversion for bicycles was introduced during repairs to an important road.

that the current model of cooperation with the city council turned to a model of systematic cooperation.

Another barrier to the popularisation of urban cycling that has been noticed by WIR is the lack of an actor that would be responsible for soft actions. Due to the perception of the cycling movement as strong and well organised, this barrier is being gradually eroded. The city council announced a competition for a cycling promotion campaign that was won by the members of Action City. The "I love Wrocław – I choose bike" campaign perfectly grasps the idea of contemporary activities of this type of cycling movement. Action City focuses on creating a positive message about cycling and showing that *normal* people – pedestrians, drivers and those who use public transport – also cycle. This message was intended to prevent antagonising different categories of road users and resulted in removing (at least partially) the stigma of a *cycling lunatic fringe* from people involved in the project and, what proved crucial in the future, people supporting the project. The stigma was partly caused by the local media presenting urban utility cyclists (as opposed to weekend, recreational cyclists) as burdensome weirdoes and partly by the public perception of the early WIR activities as environmental terrorism. Today, an important element of framing is presenting the everyday practice of cycling as a valuable experience; hence posting pictures of people commuting to work by bike and highlighting clothing problems or posting microblogs on the movement's website describing the experience of cycling, etc.

It is difficult to clearly determine the effectiveness of framing the cycling movement. There are elements of *frame bridging* because symbolic descriptions of the world-out-there created by the activists of the movement include, to some extent, popular social interpretations of reality (e.g. references to comfort, use of words that focus on individuals rather than a means of transport: *people who cycle, people in cars, people commuting on foot* rather than *cyclists, drivers* or *pedestrians* or suggestions that cycle paths increase safety for all road users, including drivers and pedestrians, rather than create a privilege for one category).

Conclusions and discussion

The analysis of the Wrocław cycling movement presented in this chapter opens up a wider and multithreaded debate centred around social change. Let us start from the cultural aspect of this change. In 2010, Mikael Colville-Andersen, an expert in the field of sustainable transport and a bike celebrity who owes this status to promoting the idea of *cycle chic* (cycling to work in an office or everyday outfit instead of Lycra), compared the Dutch attitude to bicycles to their attitude to vacuum cleaners, writing:

> We all have a vacuum cleaner, we've all learned how to use it and we all use it. But we don't go around thinking about our vacuum in the course of a day. […] We don't have a "stable" of vacuum cleaners. We don't buy vacuum cleaning clothes from our LVS or wave at other "avid" vacuum cleaning "enthusiasts" on the street. […] They're both [a vacuum cleaner and a bicycle] merely incredibly effective and useful tools for making our daily lives easier.[7]

Andersen's words provoked many comments in the cycling community, which demonstrates that bicycles and cycling in Poland are not as "natural" as vacuuming. The comments often included a question: "Why can't it be like that in Poland?" This chapter attempted to answer this question by outlining political, cultural and social contexts of changes that determine conditions of action for the cycling movement and the chances of their ideas being implemented. The diagnosed barrier is civilizational and cultural and it is related to a range of factors, including the aforementioned *social vacuum* or adjusting to the conditions of late modernity as a result of the process of political transition. It seems, therefore, that cycling as a means of transport and social-spatial practices related to it will for many years be the area of activity of urban movements oriented to increasing the importance of this mode of transport in cities and promoting a culture of sustainable mobility and urban development.

By reconstructing the anatomy and development of the Wrocław cycling movement, this chapter drew attention to social consequences of the movement's activity: added value that generates change. A significant added value can be found in the pattern of local governance in major Polish cities and the dialogue between local authorities and citizens. In recent years the activity of cycling movements has changed – from a focus on political change and the use of lobbying, informal contacts and protests in the urban space as methods of action, to greater emphasis on cultural change and promotion of sustainable transport. As a result, the conditions for actions by urban cycling movements have been dynamically transforming, which poses a question about their future. Over the course of only a decade, the aims and values of cycling movements have been partly incorporated into the political aims of the authorities. This process has been accompanied by the incorporation of cycling movement's members into municipal institutions: social councils, advisory committees, and round tables. A short time ago, the participants of Critical Mass banded together in fear of a police intervention (Wrocław) and today they are considering suspending the ride as a token of appreciation for

---

7   http://www.copenhagenize.com/2010/06/vacuum-cleaner-culture.html (accessed 16 July 2015)

the gradual realisation of their demands by the authorities (Cracow).[8] Quite recently, city officials announced that cities, unlike the countryside, are not places to cycle (Warsaw), whereas today cyclists are invited to co-create the cultural urban scene for the European Capital of Culture (Wrocław).

New urban cycling movements are today in a difficult position. Quite paradoxically, they are victims of their own success, which poses a number of questions and dilemmas for their members. They need to determine whether the favour of the authorities is associated with actual recognition of the importance of their demands and whether these demands will be included in the political agenda for longer than the next election. They also need to consider whether they should accept seats in councils and advisory boards that are offered by the authorities. To what extent does participation in these bodies contribute to increasing the influence of the movement on the exercise of power and to what extent is it maintaining the status quo under a veneer of inclusion? An acceptance of the status quo limits the role of cycling activists to mediators who improve the quality of communication between the residents and the authorities. To refuse means to choose a radical, clearly anti-system path that generates a permanent conflict. Therefore, the cycling movement faces a debate on its future: to what extent should it sharpen its political claws and point them at municipal institutions, and to what extent should it focus on non-institutional, soft cultural activities so that the residents and authorities of Wrocław treat bikes as vacuum cleaners and the members of the movement can retire? This "retirement", however, seems a distant prospect, as the life of ordinary cyclists has not changed as dramatically as have the circumstances of the activity of the cycling movement.

Calendar of Events:

2001
5 August – The Cycling Wrocław Coalition (Koalicja Rowerowy Wrocław) is formed – the first citywide organisation that represents cyclists' interests.

---

8   This decision of the cycling advocacy organisation (Kraków Miastem Rowerów) caused outrage among cyclists who have greater expectations towards the city authorities and who suggest that the members of the organisation forget that Critical Mass was not just created by them, and the participation of these dissenting voices should be taken into account.

2003

9 May – first Critical Mass ride in Wrocław; the participants are detained by the police and arrested, two participants are tried in the criminal court for assault and battery of police officers.

2005

9 June – the City Council adopts a project of developing a system of bicycle paths in Wrocław and the design and implementation standards for this system of bicycle paths in Wrocław.

2006

19 June – as a result of an internal conflict, the Cycling Coalition dissolves. Wrocław Cycling Initiative (Polish: Wrocławska Inicjatywa Rowerowa, abbreviated WIR) is formed.

2007

3 August – WIR hands over to the city president the "Golden Curb", a 45-kilogram symbol of the bicycle paths that are not in accordance with the standards adopted in 2005.

7 August – representatives of WIR meet the president and city officials. The activists propose to develop the city's bicycle policy by appointing a president's plenipotentiary for the development of bicycle transportation.

December – appointment, for the first time in Poland, of a Bicycle Officer in Wrocław.

2009

June – the first Wrocław Cycling Festival, organised by WIR.

2010

March – the estimated proportion of bicycle transportation in the entire urban traffic is 1.5%.

August – first advanced stop line in Poland is introduced in Wrocław.

14 October – the City Council adopts Urban Bicycle Policy, a policy paper for the development of bicycle transportation. This policy paper is the fulfilment of a promise made in August 2007. The Urban Bicycle Policy plans a 10% proportion of bicycles in urban traffic, increasing to 15% in 2020.

2011

22 April – WIR, together with other organisations networked in Cities for Bikes (Miasta dla Rowerów) succeed in bringing about changes in the Road Traffic Act that are favourable for cyclists.

8 June – Wrocław City Bike, a public bicycle system with 140 bicycles in 17 stations, is launched.

2012
The proportion of bicycles in the urban traffic in Wrocław is 3.56%.

2013
4 October – the Ministry of Transport appoints the first plenipotentiary for the development of bicycle transportation.

30 November – legalisation for bringing bicycles into railway stations (platforms, tunnels, halls) when the bicycle is not intended for transport.

9 November – cycling under the influence of alcohol is no longer an offence nor is it punishable by imprisonment.

2014
11 May – the President of Poland signs an amendment to the law, allowing cycling along the bank of the Odra River. In Wrocław, bicycle paths along the Odra river are key recreation areas.

September – 16,000 residents of Wrocław (10% of voters) vote for a civil project for the construction of bicycle paths in Wrocław in participatory budgeting.

October – Action City (Akcja Miasto) is formed, as a result of the success of the bicycle project in participatory budgeting.

December – Action City wins a competition announced by the City Council for a campaign promoting utility cycling under the slogan: "I love Wrocław – I choose bike".

2015
March – the Wrocław Social Diagnosis demonstrates that 0.5% of residents choose bicycle as their main means of transport (not recreation) around the city.

21 March – a family ride under the slogan: "(Not so much) Critical Mass" is organised in place of the Critical Mass. The cycling advocacy movement debates resignation from Critical Mass.

28 April – the 5th season of the Wrocław City Bike starts. The system includes 720 bicycles in 72 stations.

14 June – the city President opens the Wrocław Cycling Festival, in which 6,000 residents of Wrocław participate. Although he does not join the peloton, his deputy cycles together with his family. On the following day the President invites Wrocław cyclists to co-create bicycle culture in the city as a part of the European Capital of Culture in 2016.

Igor Pietraszewski

Artists and Power in the Field of (Subsidized) Urban Culture

Abstract: The purpose of the chapter is to analyze the relationship between power and art-ists in the field of subsidized municipal culture. The article also investigates the conversion of financial capital that take place as a consequence of awarding funds for artistic activities, organization of production and the creation of art, subjecting it to assessment and its con-version into symbolic capital. The chapter is based on the results of empirical research done with the representatives of city authorities, organizers, and artists in Wrocław. It presents the process of the conversion of capitals, in which the economic capital at the disposal of authority is converted into artistic capital, which in turn is converted into symbolic capital, serving to legitimize authority.

Keywords: cultural policy, economics, conversion of capitals, art, relationship authority-artists, Wrocław

Culture and the city

For several decades the importance of culture to the economic development, material well-being and democratization of political life has been the subject of numerous investigations, analyses and academic studies, both on the global (Harrison and Huntington 2000) and local (Majer 2014, Środa-Murawska and Szymańska 2013, Smoleń 2003a and 2003b, Klasik 2009) scale. To quote the reflec-tions of David Thorsby, culture in the functional sense may be understood as "hu-man activities which involve creativity, which are concerned with the generation and communication of symbolic meaning, and which output, at least potentially, some form of intellectual property" (Thorsby 2010: 20). As Allan J. Scott points out (2014), we are living in times of cognitive-cultural capitalism, in which culture is becoming one of the primary domains of accumulation of capital and a source of economic development. As a result it is thus becoming a phenomenon analyzed in economic terms. Similarly, Richard Florida (2002: xiii) points out that "human creativity is the ultimate economic resource" and emphasizes that it is a "virtually unlimited". Citing Florida's concept (regardless of the numerous critiques to which it has been subjected) seems relevant in so far as local authorities (Dutkiewicz 2006: 149) – in Poland and elsewhere – refer directly to his theory, using it as the basis for their cities' development strategies (Markusen *Urban Cities...*).

In Poland the links between culture, economy and creativity have also become a topic of interest to scholars from various disciplines.[1] As noted by the authors of the study entitled *Kultura a rozwój* (Culture vs. Development; Hausner, Karwieńska and Purchla 2013):

> Culture is a constituent of the social framework and at the same time an important resource upon which the economy draws, and one of the mechanisms – increasingly more important – of boosting economic development. Cultural activity requires material (economic) fueling, but at the same time, without culture, the economy could not function and grow.

Similarly, in *Odrodzenie miast* (The Revival of Cities) Andrzej Majer writes: "successful countries and cities were those where it had been possible to imagine postponed – and thus predictable – effects of development strategies focused on enriching the cultural industry (…)" (2014: 98).

Increased awareness of the economic relevance of culture results in the vital importance of cultural policy, the task of which consists of attaining the objectives of the authority by "setting directions of the development of the culture sector and amending market verdicts. The tools of intervention include financial instruments (subsidies, grants, tax exemptions) and formulation of regulations" (Towse 2011). Culture, created by the representatives of the creative class, that is those, whose "property – which stems from their creative capacity – is intangible because it is literally in their heads" (Florida 2002: 68), becomes the driving force of the economy and hope for the development of post-industrial cities. Despite a growing awareness of the significance of culture in Poland, no effective model of its financing has been developed for more than twenty years (since the socio-political transformation of the country in 1989),[2] and the national cultural policy has been "chaotic and essentially passive".[3] Researchers also emphasize the lack of "systemic changes that would be conformant with an original cultural policy, implemented consistently on the basis of a modern legal system of culture" as well as the absence of "intermediary institutions", quasi-non-government organizations (foundations, councils etc.) that would distribute the public funding allocated to

---

1 "Kultura się liczy" (Culture Counts) Campaign initiated by the National Centre for Culture in 2010.

2 As pointed out by the authors of the National Strategy for the Development of Culture for years 2004–2013, J. Głowacki, J. Hausner, K. Jakóbik, K. Markiel, A. Mituś, M. Żabiński, *Finansowanie kultury i zarządzanie instytucjami kultury*. University of Economics in Kraków, www.kongreskultury.pl/library/File/RoSK%20finansowanie_w. pelna.pdf, page 7, [accessed: 10.06.2015].

3 (Ibid., p. 6.)

culture, and the little (compared to the Western European states) autonomy of culture in Poland (Ilczuk and Nowak 2011: 88).

For the distributor of public funds, culture is not an autotelic aim – it serves pro-development purposes and is an element of a city's creation. For artists, culture (art) is the essence of creative activity and their professional life. The relations that bind representatives of the world of power and the world of art are becoming an interesting focus of considerations. As noted by the authors of the study entitled *Financing of Culture and Management of Cultural Institutions*:

> Public patronage resembles the behavior of the enlightened ruler, who allows all of his subjects to turn to him personally and who by reviewing the petitions (applications) addressed to him wants to do good. The number of petitions (applications) grows systematically, but in effect the system radically bureaucratizes and the good ruler is increasingly more separated from the people by the clerks that surround him, including those that have political empowerment and ambitions (Ilczuk, Nowak 2011: 9).

The process of conversion of capitals in the field of urban culture

This chapter aims to analyze the processes of conversion of capitals which accompany the award and consumption of public funding by the actors operating in Wrocław's urban field of culture. In order to analyze them one must – following Pierre Bourdieu's guidelines – take a closer look at the relations that connect the entities operating in the field, and investigate the process of distribution of the capitals possessed by these entities (Bourdieu, Wacquant 2001: 78). This domain is positioned at the interface of culture subsidized by public funds and the world of city politics, resulting in a specific field of cultural production. It combines the principles prevailing in the field of power with those that prevail in the world of art, where the aim lies in the production of "belief in a work of art" (Ibid.: 65) and which are "based on the principle of rejection and reversal of the law of the material benefit" (Ibid.: 78). The dominant role in this domain is played by the distributors of funds – politicians and bureaucrats – who decide on the direction of the flow of funding. A game is played between them, representatives of bohemians being the creative class (Theiss 2011: 123) (producers of artistic values), and the distributors of funding allocated to culture (the organizers of cultural life, or sometimes the artists themselves).

The research material compiled as the basis of the current analysis was collected as part of the Wrocław Social Analysis project. It consisted of twenty-eight in-depth, semi-structured interviews conducted between July and November 2014 with cultural producers – politicians, clerks, artists and organizers. They were connected by their activity in the field of culture, but divided by their position on the different rungs of the artistic, political and institutional ladders. Respondents included both accomplished artists with dominant positions in the art market, as well as novices only beginning to mark their presence. Institutional respondents included politicians and clerks creating and supervising the implementation of city's cultural policy, as well as those who carried out their assignments as part of their job in local cultural institutions. Finally, organizers (who represented both city institutions and businesses involved with culture on the free market) included those with long-standing experience and achievements in the production of re-nowned artistic projects (also including events and festivals), as well as ordinary employees of these institutions. The selection of respondents was driven by the desire to obtain the widest possible spectrum of information in order to capture the various perspectives, attitudes and strategies of action demonstrated by the actors of the field of urban culture.

Stage I: From defining the objectives of cultural policy to dispensing public funding

The functioning of subsidized urban culture is focused around two fundamental processes – the circulation of money and the circulation of symbolic values. At the first stage of the process under investigation, the key role is played by the city's distributors of public funds (clerks and politicians). It is they who define the objectives and make strategic decisions regarding the amount and the direction of the flow of funding allocated to culture. From their perspective, investing in culture serves to increase the prestige of the city and obtain an economic output by broadening the cultural offer addressed to both the residents as well as external stakeholders (including tourists). As one of the decision makers said:

> We formulated these operational and strategic objectives (…). First, for Wrocław to be an important cultural center in Central and Eastern Europe (…). The second element (…) is the creation of a musical Wrocław. It is partly connected with the large investment projects, such as the National Music Forum, that we have to somehow fill them. So it is somehow building the prestige of the city and what we offer residents through music (…). Thirdly, the offer – when we have the culture, we must prepare a weekend and summer offer. It is an element (…) of attracting people to Wrocław. It is about two challenges: the weekend is about wanting to make Wrocław Lower Silesia's capital of culture as well. So people want to come here for the weekend, because there's a theater, there's a concert, and it is profitable for the city, because usually when someone comes from Dzierżoniów, they'll have coffee etc. So this is the circulation. And during the vacation season, we also get a higher number of tourists. The fourth element is all the educational programs, which

later translate into various things. And this includes the question of the next program, which is an offer for young people.

In the opinion of the institutional respondents, the extended cultural offer becomes both a magnet that attracts a particular kind of consumer and a tool to build the prestige and create the brand of an appealing, modern and dynamic city. The city thus becomes a space for global processes such as consumerization and homogenization of culture, as well as an arena for spectacular cultural events such as festivals[4] and events and, in the process, takes on the characteristics of Western countries with well-developed cultural markets (Szlendak 2010).

In 2006 Wrocław's mayor, Rafał Dutkiewicz, wrote:

> One of Wrocław's assets are its festivals. We have several dozen of them, probably the most amongst Polish cities. By their nature, festivals bring a very broad offer, and the organizers know how to look for audiences. We try to make sure that there is no dead time in the city, each month we offer – in addition to the usual-unusual rhythm of performances, concerts, exhibitions etc. – some big attraction. The term 'off season' has become obsolete in Wrocław: the summer months are filled with cultural and entertainment propositions (Dutkiewicz 2006: 136).

In the opinion of the interviewed politicians, the growing number of investors and the many students who choose Wrocław as the place to continue their education are the indicators of success. A high-ranking clerk responsible for culture described the benefits of its development in the following way:

> We are all a beneficiaries, because a city without culture, without art events, without a certain culture has no identity. We are still building but – beginning with the decision on where to study – I think students choose a city where there is more going on, where there is more culture (…). The people who get a job here or investors, who see that things are happening in Wrocław, prefer to make their investments here (…). As for residents, it is a form of a certain activity, a certain fulfilment of needs other than just sleeping, eating and working. Residents here want to be proud of it and are proud that a lot is happening here, even when they do not partake – that's another thing. We must separate satisfaction with the fact that something is happening from satisfaction with the fact of participating in something.

As a result of either their own decisions or through the selection boards appointed by them, decision makers point to whom the funding is to be allocated via a system of subsidies, grants and subventions. The money may be distributed by

---

4   Every year there are thirty-two music festivals, eleven theatre festivals, four film festivals, seven literary festivals, six art festivals and fourteen interdisciplinary festivals in Wrocław – www.wroclaw.pl/festiwale-sztuki [accessed: 12.05.2015].

a city's cultural institution, an external entity (NGOs, foundations, associations, businesses operating on the art market, etc.) or directly by the artists. The latter is not the preferred option, as illustrated in this part of a statement by a clerk:

> (…) it happens very often that we are visited by various authors of different ideas, related to literature, theater, music, etc. And very often they are very interesting and absorbing discussions, but they usually end up with the originators being routinely sent away, so to speak, as if encouraged to look for a producer for their idea on their own, and then to have that producer come to the office. This procedure gives the clerk a guarantee, or at least some guarantee, that someone who is an expert in a given field will assess the project and decide that it is great and that it should be produced, and then they try to get the support and the money. Otherwise we would be building a structure, where the clerk would be the reviewer, and one [specialized] in all disciplines of art. (…) I really try to make sure that the artists are not the client, the partner, directly.

The decisionmakers representing the city stand as the purchasers of creations of artistic production. They trigger the flow of money to distributors, who (if they are not artists themselves) become an intermediary link between the vendee (the disposer of public funding) and the artist (the producer of artistic creations).

Stage II: From obtaining public funding to the production of artistic creations

In order to successfully compete for public funding, distributors must already take into account the objectives of the city's cultural policy at the application stage. If the distributors are organizers, and not the artists themselves, they must connect two logics – the clerical and the artistic. As Pierre Bourdieu wrote:

> These *double personages* (…) are those through whom the logic of the 'economy' penetrates to the heart of the universe of production for producers. They must therefore combine completely contradictory dispositions: economic dispositions which, in certain sectors of the field, are totally foreign to producers, and intellectual dispositions near to those of the producers whose work they can exploit only in so far as they know how to appreciate it and give it value (Bourdieu 1995).

If public funds form only a part of the amount necessary to produce and disseminate artistic values, distributors assume the risk of a project's financial success. From this point of view, considering the profitability of the initiative and the risk associated with it, the audience could consist of out-of-towners only. In the process of organization and preparation of the production of artistic goods distributors enable the transformation, or processing, of economic values into artistic creations. At this stage their task consists of preparing successful applications, effecting obtainment of financial resources and enabling the artist(s) to begin the realization of the creative process.

Stage III: From beginning production of artistic creations to their dissemination

The main problem mentioned by the surveyed artists was their poor financial standing. They expect decision makers to support the local artistic community. They negatively assessed the spending of public funds on events which do not support local artists, and which due to their mass nature were focused on indiscriminate audiences. As one of the artists noted:

> You paint using money you need to earn through something different than painting, yes, because you don't have your audience or your customers, because you have no way of acquiring them. Culture money is spent on some large events, which don't support the local artist (…).

From the point of view of the artist, competing for public funds involves a great deal of inconvenience, including the need to adjust to the ideas and rules imposed by politicians and clerks, whose cultural competences do not (in the opinion of the artists) predispose them to evaluate and judge in matters of esthetics (and thus to make financial decisions). They also mentioned the inconvenience of needing to follow formal requirements (preparing reports, observing deadlines, clearing the awarded funds, etc.).

In many cases, applying for subsidies requires artists to give up (at least part of) their artistic freedom. The distributors of public funding (politicians, clerks – be it at the local, state, or European level) devise the subjects of contests, and the artists competing for money tailor their projects to their notions. They decide to take part in the game due to the economic necessity, the opportunity to obtain funds for the realization of their own artistic projects or the legitimization of their artistic status obtained thanks to decision makers' recognition. Those artists whose position does not allow them full freedom in realizing their own artistic visions, and who are forced by the realities of everyday life to compete for funding must – as one of the respondents put it – "play somebody else's game of chess". Many artists are forced to make their living in ways not necessarily connected with art, or to shift their professional activities into entertainment or commercial and functional art. Only a few have the comfort of creating without the constraints resulting from the use of public funding, without looking at the clerks that supervise their activity, or without being guided by the expectations of the audience. On the other hand, the money received for artistic activity from the public budget is a kind of a distinction. It involves the successful passing through a verification process (amongst all those competing for the money), organized in various ways, and becomes a confirmation of the artist's value.

Stage IV: From the dissemination of artistic values to the legitimization of power

If, as an effect of the above process – composed of the decision to award the public funding made by the decision makers, the handover of the funds to the distributor and organizing the process of production – the artist has produced an artistic creation, the next stage consists of the public consumption of the creation. The artist themselves, or an organizer supervising the entire process, are the distributors responsible for the dissemination of the creation. By making the artistic product public, the creation is subjected to assessment, and the artistic value is transformed into a symbolic value.

The (not necessarily correlated) indicators of success and the consequent position of the artists in the field of urban culture come from the recognition by other (equal or better) artists, art critics and the public (which also includes the distributors of funds – economic value - who made the entire process possible).

Conversion of capitals in the field of subsidized urban culture

As an effect of such a multi-stage process, in which the aforementioned producers and actors in the field of urban culture are involved, the different capitals are converted in several steps (fig. 1). In the first stage, the disposers of public funding decide on the direction in which the money flows. Political capital is converted into economic capital. At the second stage – after the funding has been handed over to the distributor, and the artist has begun the process of producing an artistic creation – economic capital is converted into artistic capital. At the next (third) stage, when the artistic creation is made public and assessed, artistic capital is converted into symbolic capital. If the artistic creation proves to be a success, its value (symbolic capital) is converted and becomes political capital (stage four). The distributors of public funds are those who accumulate and consume political capital gained through this process. In this way, art becomes the tool that legitimizes the institutions of power. Taking into consideration the lack of an established model of financing culture in Poland, as well as practically non-existent private sponsorship possibilities and art markets (both at the institutional level as well as in the relations between the artist and the buyer) as expressed by the respondents-artists, it might be expected that the artists' economic standing would compel them to compete for public subsidies. Dependence on the city's sponsorship, which frequently becomes the only option to obtain the financial resources necessary to continue to produce art, will lead (if there are no new regulations at the state level) to further limitation of the autonomy of culture. In a system functioning in such a way artists are (and will likely continue to be) dependent on the ideas and decisions of clerks and politicians, whose cultural competences (not only in the opinion of artists) are at a level severely lower than their role in the process of making decisions regarding culture would ideally require. As such, the freedom of the artistic process will continue to be constrained by bureaucratic decisions and the subjects of the contests they devise, whose objective is not the creation of notable works of art, but rather building the image of, and legitimizing power.

Figure 1: Chart illustrating the process of conversion of capitals in the field of subsidized urban culture

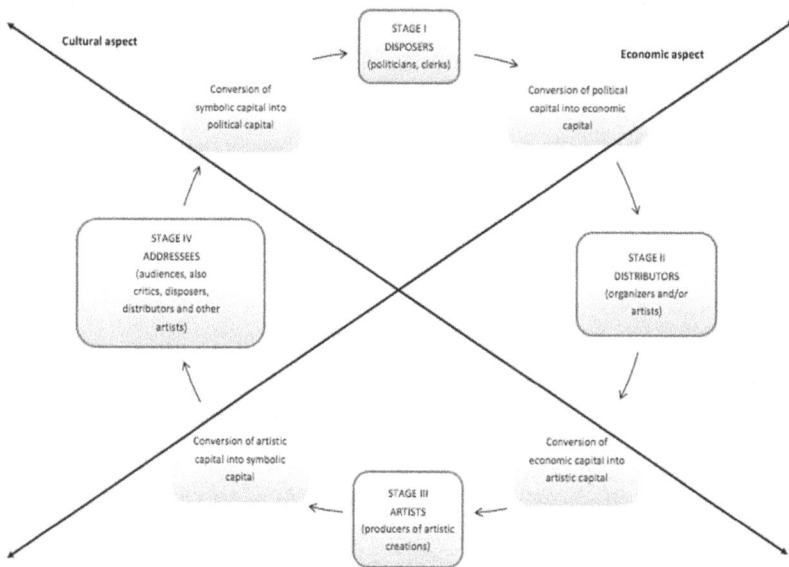

Source: Own work

Translated by Igor Pietraszewski

Mateusz Błaszczyk

The Football Paradigm in Wrocław Urban Policy: the Municipalisation of Śląsk Wrocław

Abstract: Based on analysis of the content of local newspapers, this chapter examines the history of the municipalisation of the local football club, Śląsk Wrocław. The football paradigm refers to Wrocław's urban policy, which involves the promotion of football and making it one of the city's distinguishing characteristics. The local authorities intended to integrate the residents into this football paradigm; however, they also wanted to gain legitimisation for their actions.

Keywords: football, urban policy, urban development, *scenes*, Wrocław

Introduction

At one time, there was a popular story going round the city council offices in Wrocław. It involved Turkish visitors who were invited to Wrocław when the city was applying to host the International Exposition Expo 2012. During a party that was thrown for the occasion, the atmosphere was stiff, formal and even boring. Very conventional up to a point, the conversation turned to football. One of the directors of the office and a big football fan wanted to show his knowledge on the subject and performed one of the chants of Fenerbahçe Spor Kulübü supporters. Turkish visitors, fans of Fenerbahçe, received it with applause. The ice was broken and the content Turks assured their hosts that they would support Wrocław's bid for Expo 2012 (Brzozowski 2009).

This situation may have made the Wrocław mayor realise the strength and potential of football. Shortly after, he admitted in public that "we live in a football paradigm". Implementation of this paradigm in local politics has had a profound impact on the city's development. Football has become a key factor influencing the main initiatives of the local authorities. There are at least three interlinked aspects of the football paradigm in Wrocław urban policy: 1) municipalisation of the local football club, 2) construction of a football stadium and 3) hosting UEFA Euro 2012. This chapter is dedicated to the first aspect. The involvement of local authorities in the activity of a football club is analysed to examine the characteristics of contemporary urban policy.

The city as a consumption site

A common theory in urban studies suggests that consumption is a key development factor in contemporary cities (Crewe and Beaverstock 1998; Wynne and O'Connor 1998; Glaeser at al. 2004; Clarke 2004; Jayne 2005; Glaeser and Gottlieb 2006). What is more, the growth of consumer culture is linked to surmounting the industrial city crisis, which is exemplified by the history of Detroit (Sugrue 1996) and Flint (Dandaneau 1996). In the contemporary urban discourse, urban crisis has been overtaken by *urban resurgence* (Storper and Manville 2006) or even *the triumph of the city* (Glaeser 2011).

Manuel Castells (2002) suggests that rather than from deterioration of the *framework of life*, the crisis of cities results from the deterioration of a certain idea of urban life that is expressed in everyday practices and behaviour patterns of city residents: various social groups and individuals. This crisis is a consequence of the city's failure as a system of consumption that serves to satisfy the common needs of its residents. Therefore, the core of urban resurgence is reformulation of consumption: shifting the accents from collective consumption (Saunders 1979) to individual consumption (Rogerson et al. 1996).

The starting point to understand this phenomenon is the theory of consumer society, in which consumption (possibilities and ways of consuming) is the primary objective and it organises social order, including social relations, structures, norms, customs, politics, ethics and even aesthetics (Goodwin et al. 1997; Bauman 2009). Consumption is the means and the driving force of social and economic change and an element that constructs the social meaning of space. It also plays a pivotal role in developing identity and lifestyle (Rogerson et al., 1996; Jayne 2005; Glaeser and Gottlieb 2006).

To understand the supra-individual and non-economic meanings of consumption, it is crucial to take its cultural aspects into consideration. Culture organises individual consumer practices in the form of repeatable patterns of social practices. In broader terms, it is also an essential carrier of knowledge of individual and social aspirations and needs, as well as the possibilities and methods of satisfying them. This knowledge is becoming a primary social competence – it motivates potential consumers to act and provides instructions on how to act, which allows an individual to perform the role of a consumer. The way this role is performed and the cultural pattern that is followed determine a lifestyle, of which an immanent element (in the case of consumer society, even a primary element) is the consumption style (Błaszczyk et al. 2010). Thus, consumption is not (or not only) a tool to satisfy needs, it is also (or even most of all) a tool to gather cultural capital. Therefore, it serves to build symbolic capital, in Bourdieu's terms (Featherstone

2007). By consuming cultural values, individuals appropriate elements that they use to define their social identities, i.e. to find their social position and to distinguish themselves from others (Belk et al. 1982; Wattanasuwan 2005).

Discussions about transformations of contemporary cities should be an element of a broader debate on macrosocial and macroeconomic changes that have been observed since the 1970s. Globalisation and digitalisation processes as well as transformation of the Regimes of Capital Accumulation and the development of a new, international division of labour are manifestations of these macro changes. Rich literature that is devoted to this problem uses many conceptual terms to describe aspects of this transformation, such as *post-Fordism* (Amin 1994), *postmodernism* (Harvey 1987; Jameson 1991), *liquid modernity* (Bauman 2000) and *the third wave* (Toffler 1981).

Referring to economic change in the contemporary world, Allan J. Scott (2007, 2008) suggests that capitalism has entered a new development phase that he calls *cognitive-cultural capitalism*. Economic growth is now generated by gaining competitive advantage through creativity and innovation in what Stefan Krätke (2012) calls *patent industries* and *copyright industries*. The key resource that increases city productivity growth in a cognitive-cultural economy is the high human capital of city residents (Glaeser et al. 2004: 139), i.e. a labour force with high levels of education and creativity, which are the foundation of creative industries and the knowledge-based economy.

These competences, which are particularly attractive in a contemporary economy, are described by Manuel Castells (2009) as *self-programmable labour*. They are characteristic of specific social groups that are called *Yuppie* and *Buppie* (Zukin 1998), a *metropolitan class* (Jałowiecki 2000), a *creative class* (Florida 2002) or a *world-class* (Moss Kanter 2003). Members of these groups have (1) the competence to create and use knowledge, cultural values and innovation, which are crucial in cognitive-cultural capitalism; (2) a specific lifestyle, which results from the character of their work and the essence of which is postmodern, individual consumption; and (3) a high degree of spatial mobility. The first of these characteristics results in the attractiveness and privileged position of these social categories on the job market. The second feature is related to particular, postmodern forms of consumption that mainly serve individual creation, upgrading of and communication of one's social identity (Grubb and Grathwohl 1967; Pine and Gilmour 1998). The third means that members of these groups are not spatially attached to their workplace and they can relatively freely choose their place of residence. Due to these characteristics, the discussed social categories become a subject of global competition in which cities participate. Therefore, not only do cities seek to create conditions in which knowledge and competence could endogenously emerge, they also want to gain outside human capital and keep it within their borders.

The politics of consumption as an urban policy

This chapter argues that in the face of the globalisation of capital (Harvey 1996) and the emergence of the international marketplace of cities (Savitch and Kantor, 2002), cities take on the role of a repository of resources. As a product of social relations and a form of accumulation of capital, this repository is shaped by large, transnational corporations (Błaszczyk 2013). From this perspective, for the growth of cities that want to increase their competitiveness, they need to develop social groups that have a pivotal role in cognitive-cultural economies; cities also need to obtain these groups from the outside and keep them within their borders. In this context, Terry Clark argues that the traditional paradigm, according to which job positions attract new residents, is now reversed. According to Clark, jobs are created in locations inhabited by people with competences that allow them to hold key positions in contemporary economy structures (Clark et al., 2004). To appeal to these groups, cities need to offer a high quality of life, i.e. the possibility for individuals to fulfil the sophisticated consumer needs that compose their lifestyle. In this way, these groups become privileged subjects of urban policy and create a *new knowledge aristocracy* (Shearmur 2006).

The system of consumption is an immanent element of cities. It can be understood as a functional urban product that is involved in the processes of reproduction of social resources. Its mechanisms of sharing and distribution serve to meet specific needs. The system combines three elementary elements: (1) resources, i.e. an organised team of various types of agents that specialise in meeting specific needs; (2) the actual practices of meeting needs that connect providers and consumers and (3) city users as consumers who are equipped in diverse forms of individual resources and, in their actions, transform these resources into diverse forms of capital (Błaszczyk et al. 2010:27). Politicisation of consumption treated as a driver of local development is reflected in the coherent impact of local authorities on all three elements of this system.

The first manifestation of this impact is organisation and co-creation (direct or indirect) of an *urban system of opportunities*: a group of interrelated spatial, institutional and social forms, through which resources and means of consumption are available (Błaszczyk and Cebula 2016). At the same time, the manner of organising and creating the system of opportunities favours particular styles and patterns of consumption, causing desirable social practices in public space. As a result, urban politics can be seen as local authorities' efforts to increase the volume of consumption in the social system. To meet this objective, social activation methods are employed, i.e. elements of social policy that influence lifestyles (Daly and Silver 2008; Błaszczyk at al. 2010). Moreover, there are attempts to bring new urban elites into city consumption systems because they are particularly desirable categories of consumers due to their lifestyles (Florida 2002).

In his analysis of the aforementioned mechanism, Terry N. Clark (2004b) uses a metaphor of a city as an *entertainment machine*. According to Clark, amenity-rich urban space makes a city more attractive as a place of residence, therefore driving the growth of migration, particularly of new urban elites. Simultaneously, a varied selection of leisure consumption possibilities leads to the growth of the entertainment, cultural and tourist sectors, in which many residents find employment. According to Terry N. Clark (2004a), consumer society and consumer culture are reflected in the emergence of the New Political Culture (NPC). This theory demonstrates the influence of the post-Fordist economy and postmodernist cultural order on local politics. The NPC can be perceived as a model of government that became common in the late 1980s and responded to the new needs of city residents. It was characteristic of the *New Mayors*, who went beyond traditional ideological and political differences in their management of American and Western European cities. They combined liberal social policy with conservative financial policy and innovative management methods, such as the *New Public Management* as well as a direct way of addressing voters, independently of party apparatus (Clark and Inglehart 1998).

Characteristically, the NPC moves away from the management style that takes a traditional approach to society and social divisions based on class and focuses on fiscal issues. By combining market liberalism with social progressiveness, the NPC approach breaks conventional left-right and conservatism-liberalism spectrums. This model focuses more on cultural issues, preferring them over class structure and distribution of economic values. The NPC replaces material values with post-material values, such as individual liberty and self-expression.

The New Political Culture concentrates on consumption in terms of lifestyle. Therefore, cultural issues manifested by loose, informal citizen groups, social movements, media and experts are included in the management agenda. Their role in the political discourse and their impact on decisions in the public domain is more important than the role of traditional, institutionalised structures, such as political parties, labour unions, formal organisations, etc. At the same time, the NPC is opposed to the traditional objectives of the welfare state. The effectiveness of managing public services is linked to the decentralisation of this type of management and the dispersion of these services; incorporating new subjects (e.g. due to privatisation), professionalisation and shifting of the responsibility for these services to the citizens. The NPC also increases the participation of residents in management, e.g. through fragmentation of the political agenda and emphasising *issue politics*, in which specific organisations, social movements and citizen groups are engaged (Clark and Harvey 2010).

An urban policy that leads to urban revival results from good recognition and effective satisfaction of the consumer needs of residents. As a consequence, local establishment directs its actions at the development of urban infrastructure that corresponds with consumption styles that are predominant in the social-spatial area. In other words, the policy of urban development becomes a policy of supporting certain consumption-oriented lifestyles. It is implemented by creating amenities in urban space. T.N. Clark (2004b) distinguishes four types of amenities: (1) natural physical amenities, (2) constructed amenities, (3) socio-economic composition and diversity, and (4) values and attitudes of residents.

A specific configuration of these types of amenities in a certain socio-geographic area – a unique, local *amenities basket* – determines the attractiveness of a city. From an urban policy perspective, constructed amenities are of particular importance as they can be directly controlled by local authorities. Local authorities can relatively easily and quickly create, or support the creation of amenities that enhance the quality of life of certain groups of residents-consumers. These amenities are in the form of spatial structures, institutions or events that construct urban systems of opportunities. Activities that support the system of consumption (its forms as well as legitimisation and stimulation of desirable patterns of consumer behaviour) can be considered a political emanation of rules that organise the consumer society.

The model of a city as an entertainment machine in the postmodern culture of consumption – the new city elites' domain – usually wins considerable social acceptance, thus it increases popularity and support for the local authorities. At the same time, the development of amenities characteristic of postmodern, individualistic and post-material consumption legitimises symbolic domination of the creative urban elite.

The entertainment machine needs a continuous power supply – consumers. Therefore, urban politics is increasingly more intensively directed at producing and promoting new forms of entertainment, which are often enriched by cultural aspects. Consumption of leisure contributes to the revival of urban life, which is expressed in the saturation of urban space with social activities for consumers. From this perspective, an attractive city is a city with a broad range of consumption activities and various forms of leisure; a city in which residents can feel like tourists. Therefore, local authorities often support the organisation of various events that are believed to make cities desirable destinations for *cultural tourism* (Richards and Palmer 2010; Smith and Richards 2013).

Amenities do not function independently or autonomously in urban structures. They cluster into what Daniel Silver, Terry Clark and Clemente Yanez (2010) call *scenes*. The concept of scenes is a theoretical tool that combines spatial forms, structural social diversity and lifestyles expressed in consumption and participation in urban life. In this approach, culture consumption can be analysed as an organised, actualised and spatially situated social activity with a multi-level and diverse structure. The concept of *scenes* helps to explain different patterns of consumption in urban space and the social consequences of these differences.

This concept highlights specific locations, spatial forms and the configuration of institutions and social activities in which cultural practices are manifested. Scenes are aimed at providing experiences (Pine and Gilmour 1998) and socialising individual activities. Thus, scenes conglomerate citizens-consumers on the basis of similarities in their lifestyle and sensibility. Scenes consolidate: (1) groups of citizens who share particular lifestyles, (2) spatial forms that serve specific consumption practices and (3) experiences that are characteristic of consumption styles provided by scenes. In other words, opportunities for consumption and acts of consumption that happen in contact with others and are available in specific sites (e.g. in restaurants, cafes, shops, theatres, etc.), determine the scope of the experiences and values obtained in the consumption process. This process is the essence of forming urban *scenes*. Therefore, *scenes* may be considered elements of urban structure that organise urban consumption opportunities. By gathering an audience – consumers – they provide them with specific forms of consumption and symbolic values. Thus, *scenes* mediate urban opportunities of leisure consumption. They are also an area of forming an audience, e.g. a new element of social structure that includes social, economic, demographic and cultural characteristics of the participants of the scene. The concept of a *scene* is thus an interesting analytical tool, which helps to overcome the limitations of traditional terms that serve to describe and explain the complexity of urban structures and urban life.

Municipalisation of Śląsk Wrocław

Based on press reports, this chapter reconstructs and analyses the public discourse about the transfer of Śląsk Wrocław football club to municipal ownership. This process is presented as an element of a wider policy, defined here as the *football paradigm*. The case of Śląsk Wrocław is used as an empirical example of a political construction of an urban *scene*, through which ideological fundaments of the New Political Culture manifest themselves.

The history of Śląsk Wrocław goes back to 1946. In 1964 the club was promoted to the top football league in Poland and was the biggest and most important football club in the town. Founded as a military club, Śląsk Wrocław enjoyed its greatest sport successes in the late 1970s and early 1980s, when it finished in the top three on five occasions, and won the league in 1977. It also performed well in the Polish Cup and in the European Cup and UEFA Cup. The U-19 team also achieved good results. These successes resulted in increased interest in football among Wrocław inhabitants and record attendances for games.

The club's situation deteriorated in the 1990s after the political transition in Poland. The military department was no longer interested in investing in the club and it did not have the financial resources necessary for sporting successes. In 1997 the football section (to which the league team belonged) was separated from the multi-sport military club (Wojskowy Klub Sportowy) and its name changed to Wrocławski (*of Wrocław*, instead of Wojskowy-*Military*) Klub Sportowy Śląsk Wrocław (WKS). The poor financial situation, increasing debt, the consequences of involvement in a corruption scandal and poor sporting results almost led to the downfall of the club. In the 2002–2003 season, WKS was relegated to the third division. Games against little-known provincial clubs did not attract the interest of the residents of Wrocław, and attendances dwindled.

In the face of this situation, in the first decade of the 21st century, the idea of the communalisation of Śląsk Wrocław was discussed for the first time by city officials. An additional impetus was the decision to apply to host the 2012 UEFA European Football Championship and, consequently, to build a large new stadium that would become the home stadium of Śląsk Wrocław after the tournament.

The communalisation involved buying the shares owned by the private company that ran the club, financing the club and making it the main tenant of the new stadium and, in the long term, finding a private co-owner and investor. These measures were intended to help the club gain promotion to the first division, become one of the leaders in the league and subsequently play in European club competitions. At a conference devoted to the city plans concerning WKS, the director of the city council department of social affairs presented the following vision of Wrocław's club future and the future of Wrocław football in general: "We believe in miracles. We also dream of qualification for the UEFA Champions League; simultaneously, we are applying to host the 2012 European Championship and we're going to build a modern football stadium, which will be finished in four years. Everything is really nicely falling into place" (Brzozowski 2006).

The decision to communalise the football club and make it the sporting show-case of Wrocław met general acceptance and even enthusiasm from the city's politicians, the local media and the citizens. It was even supported by the council-lors opposed to the government in power: "I would like to congratulate the local government on the firm and right decision. I share your optimism (…) because Wrocław is a European city and it has the potential to build a strong football club"; "I am happy to hear of the mayor's intention to finally rebuild football in Silesia. I have waited for two terms to hear it at last. This is a brilliant idea" (Brzozowski 2006). Journalists and Wrocław inhabitants who commented on these events on the internet were also enthusiastic.

The communalisation of the club soon brought measurable organisational and sporting effects. The owner of the club – a rich and high-ranked city – guaranteed stability and credibility, which facilitated acquiring sponsors, including state and communal companies. In 2008, the state monopolist on the energy market, the Energia Pro concern, became the main sponsor, while a communal company established to build the stadium became the title sponsor.

Śląsk Wrocław won promotion to the first division in the 2007–2008 season. The following year, it won the League Cup and in the 2010–2011 season it was runner-up in the league. The following season brought the greatest successes: the national championship, the Polish Super Cup, and getting into the third qualifica-tion round of the Champions League. A year afterwards the club again performed well (third place) and played well in the UEFA Europa League.

The city's ownership and, since 2009, co-ownership (after selling 51% of the shares to a private holder) of Śląsk Wrocław resulted in a considerable increase in direct and indirect financial transfers (through communal companies) from the city budget to the club. One of the consequences of the radical increase in spending on the football club was a reduction in funding for other sporting dis-ciplines, including a very popular and successful men's basketball team. Annual, multimillion-zloty subsides to Śląsk Wrocław became a permanent element of the budgetary policy. Financial transfers from the city budget to the club's came in a variety of forms: direct subventions, loans, grants (which required conditions that only Śląsk Wrocław met), money from the city promotion fund, sponsorship of municipal companies or advertising fees for the events organised by the lo-cal government. There was a very controversial situation in 2013 when MPWiK Wrocław, a municipal water supply company, gave a 4 million-zloty loan to the club on very favourable terms, and then audaciously explained that increased water and sewage charges for the general public resulted from the need to expand the water supply network (Harkułowicz 2013).

Another example of a public money transfer to the club was the contracting of WKS for marketing services, which was bizarre from the point of view of business effectiveness. The municipal Youth Sports Centre paid about 1 million zloty to Śląsk Wrocław for the promotion of the Wrocław Marathon. The advertising campaign lasted two months and was featured at four games at the city stadium. The details of the contract between the sponsor (an entity dependent on the city) and the club (led by a company whose main stakeholder was the city) provoked widespread criticism. The critics pointed out the absurdity of such a marketing strategy, particularly its huge costs (in general, 1 million is around 20–25% of the advertising budget of most major Polish cities), the low effectiveness of the selected form of promotion, the inadequate target group and the low economic efficiency: the tax on the operation may have been as much as 185,000 zloty (Wolski 2014). As it would be difficult to find a business explanation of the discussed contract, one of the commentators summarised the situation as follows: "The advertisement was only an excuse to be able to transfer money from one municipal company to another. It demonstrates the city's hopelessness in its search for a serious investor to fund the club (Skrzyński 2014).

The local authorities could legally grant a subsidy to the club directly from the city budget. Moreover, subsidies are exempt from value added tax. However, the local government is obliged to reveal information related to subsidies to sports clubs, including the amount of the subsidy and the identity of the beneficiary. Advertising expenditures, on the other hand, particularly those coming from entities dependent on the city, are not listed in the budget: the actual amounts received by the beneficiaries do not appear. Therefore, one might assume that the complex financial operation of transferring money to WKS via the Youth Sport Centre, under the guise of advertising their sporting event, was aimed at hiding from the public the real total of the city's expenditure on the club (Wolski 2014).

The football paradigm as a political narrative

The project of the communalisation of Śląsk Wrocław was presented as an element of a broader strategy for making the city more competitive. Other elements of this strategy included applying to host games in the UEFA 2012 European Championship and building a new stadium. Without a large, modern stadium, Wrocław would not have had a chance of hosting Euro 2012 matches. Its construction was also justified by the great aspirations of Śląsk Wrocław, for whom it would be a home stadium. The football paradigm included three interrelated objectives of the urban policy: (1) a European-level football club that would represent the aspirations of the city and its residents; (2) a modern stadium considered to be substantial evidence of the city's power and (3) hosting UEFA Euro 2012 matches, which was seen as a symbol of Wrocław's promotion to the "first division of European cities". One should note that the authorities' decision to enter the football business was more than just another aspect of the commercialisation of football as a form of entertainment (Antonowicz et. al. 2015). It was also an element of the city development strategy that was independent from the actions and efforts of autonomous football structures.

The football paradigm fitted into the overall narrative of urban development based on mega-events (Burbank et al. 2002). This approach to Wrocław's development was reinforced by applying to host EXPO 2010 and 2012 (of which Wrocław citizens generally approved). The discourse justifying this policy focuses on promotion of the city as the main benefit. Through football – the strong football team, UEFA Euro 2012 and, indirectly, the new stadium – it was believed that Wrocław would increase and reinforce its international status. The city's position in football was intended to increase its recognisability and develop its positive image. This was expected to attract potential investors and tourists and, consequently, boost the local economy. Thus, the football club was perceived as a tool of territorial marketing, which was expected to bring profits to the city and its residents. In this context, the local authorities often referred to their efforts to host EXPO as an example of successful territorial marketing. The competition between Wrocław and a Korean city, Yeosu, was believed to be an important factor that helped to attract a large investor, LG Corporation (*Wrocław znów stara się o Expo* 2006). The perception of the role of a football club as a marketing tool might have been strengthened by the fact that many Wrocław citizens gained the majority of their information about many Polish towns from media reports on their respective football clubs. From this perspective, the status of a city is reduced to the local football club's stature.

Not only were communalisation of the club and the construction of a new stadium seen as necessary steps to apply to host UEFA Euro 2012, they were also considered an investment in the development of the city. Hosting Euro 2012 was seen as a chance for a "civilisational jump" that would help Wrocław achieve the status of a truly European city, and was believed to be a guarantee of investment in infrastructure that was necessary for the city to function, e.g. a ring road, new tram lines, the airport and a modernised railway infrastructure as well as tourist accommodation (Skorupka and Górski 2010). With regard to the 2010 FIFA World Cup, the perception of this mega-event as a chance to reduce civilizational dissonance was also an important narrative that accompanied its organisation (Bob and Swart 2009; Haferburg 2011). It should be noted that the promise of the benefits that Euro 2012 was expected to bring was used as a justification for the city's financial support for Śląsk Wrocław.

Interestingly, the entire debate about football in Wrocław, particularly about the communalisation of the club, lacked arguments for increasing and improving the opportunities for leisure consumption. The public saw the local government's involvement in the football club in terms of prestige, image and marketing advantages that were supposed to serve the city (as a general public good) rather than individual citizens. At most, the club's devoted fans were the direct beneficiaries of this policy. However, even this group cared more about the club's potential league position than the quality of the football on offer. A similar diagnosis was established in later research about the social perception of the European Capital of Culture: Wrocław 2016 project (Błaszczyk 2015). This project was perceived as an event that should bring both profit and tourists to the city (Schmidt and Skowrońska 2012) while potential benefits to the citizens were considered "a side effect".

The audience of the football scene

As the owner of the club, the local authorities faced a new challenge of key economic importance: they needed to provide an audience for the football games. Increased attendance at football games was needed to obtain the financing necessary for running the club and, most of all, for the upkeep of the newly built stadium with a capacity of 45,000, which is also owned by the city. According to transfermarkt.de data, in the 2007–2008 season, after the communalisation of the club, which was then in the second division, the average game attendance was a little over 5,000. After the promotion to the first division (Ekstraklasa), between 2008 and 2011, the attendance increased. In the 2009–2010 season, the average attendance was 5,500 and a year later the number grew to 7,500. The 2011–2012 season, when the new stadium was opened and the club won the championship, pushed the attendance to record levels. The average number of spectators was 17,110, which means that about 37% of seats were occupied on average. A year later every third seat was occupied and in the following seasons the attendance was about 10,000 (Kościółek 2014).

The new stadium as the home ground of Śląsk Wrocław and the club's promotion to the first division resulted in a new element of urban policy: stimulating interest in football. Various entities dependent on the local government, including municipal agencies (e.g. the Centre for Information and Social Development), companies (e.g. the Municipal Transport Company) and schools were involved in developing a football boom. The policy involved promoting football games as an attractive form of family entertainment. Considerable discounts for family tickets and free public transport to the stadium for Śląsk Wrocław games were intended as encouragement. In 2015, in the face of dropping attendances, a promotional campaign: "No ifs or buts – #everyone4Śląsk" was launched, in which coaches, players and famous Wrocław inhabitants encouraged people to attend games (#WszyscyZaŚląskiem).

Young people were targeted as the decisive demographic that would help make football fashionable. Special campaigns encouraged chanting at the stadium. One of them, "Kids at the stadium – let's learn how to chant" involved free entrance to football games and lessons on how to cheer in an appropriate way, were organised for schools, children's sport clubs and educational facilities (*Dzieci na stadionie...*, 2015). Players visited educational facilities, including schools in towns near Wrocław, and talked to the students. In 2012 they met about 5,000 students as an element of the campaign "Śląsk Wrocław in your school" (*Piłkarze Śląska w tym roku...*, 2012). These football campaigns organised by municipal bodies were not limited to support for Śląsk Wrocław. During Euro 2012, entire school classes went to open training sessions of the Czech national football team, who were preparing for the tournament in Wrocław. The Japan-Brazil friendly organised in Wrocław was also intended to promote football in the city. To ensure a high attendance, the mayor offered tickets to the game to Wrocław schools at a reduced price. The school that bought the most tickets was promised a visit by the Brazilian team (Kozioł 2012).

Popularisation of football by locating sport events in the city was not limited to the Japan-Brazil friendly. After the 2012 European Championship, Wrocław organised (and financed) the summer Polish Masters tournament. Śląsk Wrocław and three international clubs – PSV Eindhoven, Athletic Bilbao and Sport Lisboa e Benfica – participated. However, despite their commercial character, both the tournament and the friendly ended in a financial disaster and financial losses that were covered by the city budget (Pluta 2012; Rybak and Torz 2012). The Polish Masters was followed by financial and political scandal. Poor sales of tickets for the tournament, which was broadcast on TV, provoked concerns about tarnishing the image of the local government. Therefore, a decision was taken to distribute several thousand tickets for free, which aggravated financial losses. The organisers, however, emphasised that their priority was to attract a high attendance for the event and promote the tournament. The head of the company that organised the tournament at the request of the authorities said: "Discounts on the tickets were intended to attract fans to the stadium. It was the first edition of the Polish Masters and, above all, we wanted to let people know that this event is taking place in Wrocław and that we want it to be a recurring event. It is also important that visiting football clubs leave the city with positive impressions. A positive opinion about us is a future asset" (Karbowiak 2012). It should be added that after the fiasco of the endeavour and its political repercussions (dismissals in the city management and severe criticism of the local government and the efficiency of its actions), there was no subsequent edition of the tournament.

The political roles of football

The activities of the Wrocław authorities that are discussed in this chapter display the typical elements of a new kind of social policy aimed at stimulating social activity by building social and cultural capital rather than redistributing goods in order to reduce social exclusion. In this approach, the development of mainstream lifestyles becomes the subject of social policy (Daly and Silver 2008). The authorities decided to create a scene that was intended to integrate and institutionalise (1) football as a form of urban spectacle; (2) the stadium as a site of particular forms of consumption and (3) the audience. The organisation of a football event as a form of leisure consumption was intended to give purpose to this scene. The event was believed to integrate the city's audience and popularise a lifestyle oriented at accumulation and social sharing of experiences that build the individual social and cultural capitals of citizens.

However, the football paradigm as an urban policy needs a wider interpretation. The analysis of narratives about football in Wrocław indicates several significant benefits brought about by the local authorities' actions.

First of all, the football paradigm clarified and targeted the aspirations of the city and provided a reference point for the aspirations of its inhabitants. These aspirations could be summarised as Europeanisation of Wrocław, i.e. elimination of the dissonance between the post-transition city (struggling with the consequences of the socio-economic transition from a socialist planned economy to a capitalist free market economy) and efficiently functioning, rich and developed cities of Western Europe, perceived as points of reference and role models (Błaszczyk and Pluta 2015). In this narrative, Wrocław is on its way to becoming an important city on the European map and it deserves this status for its history, tradition, potential and current transformations. In 2006, the deputy mayor, who is responsible for social affairs, perfectly manifested this attitude in his words: "Wrocław is a dynamic European city and it should have a good football team" (Brzozowski 2006).

Secondly, the ambitious challenge faced by the city integrates and mobilises the local community. The narrative about football has an inclusive character: it integrates a great number of inhabitants who adopt it as their own. This is reflected in the broad acceptance of the objectives set by the local government and the active support for the ideas promoted by the authorities (Głowacka 2006). The authorities often used this support (e.g. by organising events for citizens that were intended to demonstrate social activity; Nowaczyk 2007) as an argument in their efforts to host Expo and Euro 2012.

Thirdly, the discussed narrative legitimises governmental actions and creates political support in elections. The debate on the communalisation of Śląsk Wrocław began before the local elections in 2006, and was followed by a victory for the incumbent mayor, who won almost 85% of the votes, and victory for the ruling coalition with an absolute majority of seats in the City Council. The local authorities in fact adopted a policy of financing sporting events, which was intended to generate public approval.

Moreover, a specific division of urban issues into two spheres can be observed. One of them is the public sphere, which is concerned with the city as a generalised public good. The narrative in this sphere focuses on Wrocław's successes, dynamic development and Europeanisation and creates an image of the city that the inhabitants are proud of and with which they like to identify. The New Political Culture fits in this narrative.

The other is the sphere of everyday life, which exposes numerous inconveniences and problems related to collective consumption. It is a characteristic of neoliberalism that these problems are privatised and become problems of specific groups of inhabitants. Urban policy withdraws from managing these matters, ceding the responsibility to those who are affected by them. For instance, while the football club is considered an urban issue (e.g. in the context of the prestige, promotion, and development of the city), the problem of overcrowded kindergartens is defined as the parents' problem and the cost of housing is the problem of those who want to buy or rent accommodation. It seems that the new political culture provides approval for these phenomena. The political successes of the local authorities (to a certain point, at least) demonstrate that there is public acceptance of focusing urban policy on postmodern, individual consumption at the expense of the problems of the system of collective consumption that is mediated in specific city spaces by specific groups of inhabitants. The discussed example of the football paradigm provides reasons to conclude that the New Political Culture makes a travesty of the Ancient Roman *panem et circenses*: the rulers will provide the circuses while the citizens need to take care of their bread.

Summary

There is one thing that still needs an explanation. The analyses presented in this chapter relate to the period of development and triumph of the football paradigm but the domination of this paradigm did not last long. The crisis and decline of this formula in Wrocław urban policy would demand a separate analysis. Therefore, I will only briefly present certain facts that demonstrate the relationship between football and Wrocław urban policy.

First of all, the local authorities were criticised for financing the club from the urban budget. This problem was an important element of the political discourse during the local election campaign in 2014. The incumbent mayor, who had to date been re-elected twice, both times with a crushing majority, this time needed a second round, which was interpreted as a yellow card for his urban policy.

Although originally the communalisation project assumed later re-privatisation of Śląsk Wrocław, the local authorities did not look for a buyer until 2015, when there was an intensive search for a purchaser who would buy 49% of the shares and take over responsibility for the club. Financing from the city budget to the club was gradually reduced. While it was 16 million zloty in 2014, in 2015 the amount decreased to 6 million and a year later, to 3 million (Brzozowski 2015). Meanwhile the club lost its main sponsor (*Tauron rozstaje się...* 2014), which additionally worsened its financial situation. Moreover, key players left the club. This resulted in a downturn in sporting fortunes (around halfway though the 2015–2016 season Śląsk were at the bottom of the table) and interest was decreasing among fans. The average attendance for home games in autumn 2015 was below 8,000 (Staszak 2015). This statistic raised questions about the purpose of building the new stadium, costing almost a billion zloty, the maintenance of which is a constant drain on finances.

Negotiations with co-owners of the club about buying shares from the city started in late 2015, but failed. What is more, the consortium of private shareholders decided to resell their shares to the city. Thus, the club is now completely re-communalised. When the press revealed these negotiations, their failure and the tensions between the city and private shareholders (Gulder 2016), the authorities issued a statement in which they bragged that since they had sold shares to private holders two years earlier, they had transferred about 25 million zloty to the club (*Władze miasta odpierają zarzuty konsorcjum...*, 2016).

In fact, the authorities became victims of their own politics. In the face of decreasing interest in the games and lack of potential investors, the financial responsibility for the club falls on the city. Their withdrawal from financing and leaving the club to its own fortunes would lead to relegation and to a spectacular failure of the urban policy of last years.

The fiasco of the football paradigm, however, did not result in abandoning the *festivalisation policy* (Häußermann and Siebel 1993) that focuses on organising huge cultural and sporting events. On the contrary, in 2016 Wrocław was chosen as the European Capital of Culture and in 2017 the city will host the World Games: an international event for sports and disciplines that are not contested in the Olympic Games. However, these events do not generate as much public enthusiasm as the communalisation of Śląsk Wrocław and hosting Euro 2012 did. On the contrary, these initiatives meet considerable criticism. The controversies over the *festivalisation policy* provoked the local authorities to organise a local referendum on whether Wrocław should apply in future to host international sporting and cultural events, such as the 2016 European Capital of Culture and the 2017 World Games. Almost 72% answered yes, but the turnout was only 11%.

Bibliography

Althusser, L. (2006). "Ideology and Ideological State Apparatuses". In A. Sharma & A. Gupta (eds.), *The Anthropology of the State. A Reader*, Oxford: Blackwell.

Amin, A. (ed.) (1994). *Post-Fordism*. Oxford: Blackwell.

Andrzejewski, T. (2014). "Kliktywista potrzebny od zaraz". In M. Bukowiecki et al. (eds.), *Miasto na żądanie. Aktywizm, polityki miejskie, doświadcenia*, Warsaw: WUW.

Antoniewicz, D., Kossakowski, R., & Szlendak, T. (2015). *Aborygeni i konsumenci. O kibicowskiej wspólnocie, komercjalizacji futbolu i stadionowym apartheidzie.* Warsaw: Wydawnictwo Instytutu Filozofii i Socjologii Polskiej Akademii Nauk.

Antonowicz, D. & Wrzesiński, Ł. (2009). "Kibice jako wspólnota niewidzialnej religii". *Studia Socjologiczne*, 1(192), 115–149.

Assmann, A. (2013). *Miedzy historią a pamięcią. Antologia*. Warsaw: WUW.

Bauman, Z. (2000). *Liquid modernity*. Cambridge: Polity Press.

Bauman, Z. (2007). *Consuming life*. Cambridge: Polity Press.

Belk, R. W., Bahn, K. D., & Mayer, R. N. (1982). "Developmental recognition of consumption symbolism". *Journal of consumer research*, 9(1), 4–17.

Benevolo, L. (1995). *Miasto w dziejach Europy*. Warsaw: Volumen.

Błaszczyk, M. & Cebula, M. (2016). "Uczestnictwo w kulturze a uczestnictwo w mieście. O kapitałach kulturowych i różnorodności stylów życia mieszkańców dużego miasta". *Studia Socjologiczne*, 220(1), 99–126.

Błaszczyk, M. & Pluta, J. (2015). "Wprowadzenie. *Drugie miasto* jako przedmiot badań socjologicznych". In M. Błaszczyk, J. Pluta (eds.), *Uczestnicy, konsumenci, mieszkańcy. Wrocławianie i ich miasto w oglądzie socjologicznym*, Warsaw: Wydawnictwo Naukowe Scholar, 7–15.

Błaszczyk, M. (2013). *W poszukiwaniu socjologicznej teorii rozwoju miast. Meandry ekonomii politycznej*. Warsaw: Wydawnictwo Naukowe Scholar.

Błaszczyk, M. (2015). "Uprzemysłowienie miasta postfordowskiego jako problem polityczny". *Folia Sociologica*, no. 2.

Błaszczyk, M. (2015). "Zanim kurtyna pójdzie w górę. Reprodukcja miejskiego spektaklu w kontekście Europejskiej Stolicy Kultury Wrocław 2016". In M. Błaszczyk & J. Pluta (eds.), *Uczestnicy, konsumenci, mieszkańcy. Wrocławianie i ich miasto w oglądzie socjologicznym*, Warsaw: Wydawnictwo Naukowe Scholar, 16–58.

Błaszczyk, M., Kłopot, S., & Pluta, J. (2010). *Stare i nowe problemy społeczne wielkiego miasta. Socjologiczne studium konsumpcji na przykładzie Wrocławia.* Warsaw: Wydawnictwo Naukowe Scholar.

Bob, U., & Swart, K. (2009). "Resident perceptions of the 2010 FIFA Soccer World Cup stadia development in Cape Town". *Urban Forum,* 20(1), 47–59.

Bodnar, J. E. (1992). *Remaking America: Public memory, commemoration, and patriotism in the twentieth century.* Princeton, NJ.: Princeton University Press.

Bourdieu, P. & Wacquant, L.C. (2001). *Zaproszenie do socjologii refleksyjnej.* Transl. A. Sawisz. Warsaw: Oficyna Naukowa.

Bourdieu, P. (1995) *The rules of art. Genesis and structure of the literary field.* Stanford, California: Stanford University Press.

Boyer, C.M. (1996). *The city of collective memory: its historical imagery and architectural entertainments.* Cambridge: MIT Press.

Brown S. (2007). *Football fans around the world: from supporters to fanatics.* London-New York: Routledge.

Burbank, M. J., Andranovich, G., & Heying, C. H. (2002). "Mega-events, urban development and public policy". *Review of policy research,* 19(3), 179–202.

Cassirer, E. (1965). *The philosophy of symbolic forms. Vol. 2: Mythical thought.* New Haven and London: Yale University Press.

Castells, M. (1983). *The city and the grass roots: a cross-cultural theory of urban social movements.* Los Angeles, Berkeley: University of California Press.

Castells, M. (2002). *Collective consumption and urban contradictions in advanced capitalism.* In I. Susser (ed.), *The Castells reader on cities and social theory,* Oxford: Blackwell.

Castells, M. (2009). *Communication power.* Oxford: Oxford University Press.

Castells, M. (2011). *The rise of the network society: The information age: Economy, society, and culture* (Vol. 1). Wile: New York.

Castells, M. (2012). *Networks of outrage and hope.* Oxford: Polity Press.

Castells, M. (1989). *The informational city: information, technology, economic restructuring and the urban-regional process.* Oxford: Basil Blackwell.

Chabros, E. & Kmita, G., (2011). *Graffiti w PRL.* Wrocław: IPN.

Chabros, E. (2011). "Polskie graffiti lat osiemdziesiątych w świetle relacji jego twórców". *Pamięć i Sprawiedliwość,* 10/1(17), 211–230.

Chabros, E. (ed.) (2014). *Od kontrkultury do New Age. Wybrane zjawiska społeczno – kulturowe schyłku PRL i ich korzenie.* Warsaw: IPN.

Chłopek, M. (2004). *Bikiniarze. Pierwsza polska subkultura.* Warsaw: Żak.

Cichocki, M. (2005). *Władza i pamięć: o politycznej funkcji historii*. Cracow: Ośrodek Myśli Politycznej.

Clark, T. N. (2004a). Political theory of consumption. In T.N. Clark (ed.), *The City as an Entertainment Machine*, Bingley: Emerald Group Publishing.

Clark, T. N. (2004b). "Urban Amenities: Lakes, Opera, and Juice Bars Do They Drive Development?" In T.N. Clark (ed.), *The City as an Entertainment Machine*, Bingley: Emerald Group Publishing.

Clark, T. N. (ed.) (2011). *The City as an Entertainment Machine*. New York: Lexington Books.

Clark, T. N., & Harvey, R. (2010). "Urban politics". In *Handbook of Politics*. New York: Springer.

Clark, T. N., Lloyd, R., Wong, K. K., & Jain, P. (2002). "Amenities drive urban growth". *Journal of urban affairs*, 24(5), 493–515.

Clark, T. N., Lloyd, R., Wong, K., & Jain, P. (2004). "Amenities drive urban growth: a new paradigm and policy linkages". In T.N. Clark (ed.), *The City as an Entertainment Machine*, Bingley: Emerald Group Publishing.

Clark, T.N., & Inglehart R. (1998). "The new political culture: changing dynamics of support for the welfare state and other policies in postindustrial societies". In T.N. Clark, & V. Hoffmann-Martinot (eds.), *The New Political Culture*, Boulder, CO: Westview Press.

Clarke, D. B. (2004). *Consumer Society and the Post-modern City*. London-New York: Routledge.

Cohen, P.S. (1969). "Theories of Myth". *Man: New Series*, 4(3), 337–353.

Conway, M. A. (1997). "The inventory of experience: memory and identity". In D. Jodelet, J. Pennebaker, & D. Paez (Eds.), *Political events and collective memories*. London-New York: Routledge.

Corning, A., & Schuman, H. (2015). *Generations and collective memory*. Chicago: University of Chicago Press.

Crewe, L., & Beaverstock, J. (1998). "Fashioning the city: cultures of consumption in contemporary urban spaces". *Geoforum*, 29(3), 287–308.

Czajkowski, P. & Pabjan, B. (2013). "Pamięć zbiorowa mieszkańców Wrocławia a stosunek do niemieckiego dziedzictwa miasta". In J. Juchnowski & R. Wiszniowski (eds.), *Współczesna teoria i praktyka badań społecznych i humanistycznych. Vol. 1*, Torun: Wydawnictwo Adam Marszałek.

Czerner, O. (2011). "Odbudowa miasta po II wojnie światowej". In *Leksykon architektury Wrocławia*, Wrocław: Via Nova.

Daly, M., & Silver, H. (2008). "Social exclusion and social capital: A comparison and critique". *Theory and society*, 37(6), 537–566.

Dandaneau, S. P. (1996). *A town abandoned: Flint, Michigan, confronts deindustrialization*. New York: SUNY Press.

Davies, N., & Moorhouse, R. (2002). *Microcosm: A Portrait of a Central European City*. London: Random House.

Diani, M. (1992). "The concept of social movement". *The Sociological Review*, 40(1), 1–25.

Dobesz, J. L. (1998). "Architektura użyteczności publicznej z okresu III Rzeszy we Wrocławiu". In J. Rozpędowski (ed.), *Architektura Wrocławia, Vol. 4 Gmach*, Wrocław: Materiały Sesji Naukowej Instytutu Historii Architektury, Sztuki i Techniki Politechniki Wrocławskiej.

Dobesz, J.L. (1999). *Wrocławska architektura spod znaku swastyki na tle budownictwa III Rzeszy*. Wrocław: Oficyna Wydawnicza PWr.

Domański, H. (2002). *Polska klasa średnia*. Wrocław: Ossolineum.

Domański, H. (2005). "The Polish Transformation Structural Changes and New Tensions". *European Journal of Social Theory*, 8(4), 453–470.

Domański, H. (2012). *Prestiż*. Torun: UMK.

Dubey, A.K. (2006). "The Rickshaw Refuses to Go Away: the struggle of the cotraveller of Asian Modernity". In R. Ravi (ed.), *The Saga of Rickshaw*, Delhi: VAK.

Dudała, J. (2004). *Fani – chuligani. Rzecz o polskich kibolach. Studium socjologiczne*. Warsaw: Żak.

Durkheim, E. (1955). *Pragmatism and Sociology*. Camgridge: Camgridge Univesrsity Press.

Dutkiewicz, R. (2006). *Nowe Horyzonty*. Warsaw: Rosner & Wspólnicy.

Eliade, M. 1963. *Myth and Reality*. Jarper and Rwo: NY.

Fałkowski, M. & Popko, A. (2006b). *Niemcy o Polsce i Polakach 2000 – 2006. Główne wnioski z badania*. Warsaw: Instytut Spraw Publicznych.

Fałkowski, M. & Popko, A. (2006a) (eds.). *Polacy i Niemcy. Wzajemny wizerunek po rozszerzeniu Unii Europejskiej*. Warsaw: Instytut Spraw Publicznych.

Fałkowski, M. & Popko, A. (2006c). *Polacy w oczach Niemców 2000–2006*. In Idem, *Polacy i Niemcy. Wzajemny wizerunek po rozszerzeniu Unii Europejskiej*, Warsaw: Instytut Spraw Publicznych.

Fatyga, B. (1993). *Dzicy z naszej ulicy. Antropologia kultury młodzieżowej*. Warsaw: Ośrodek Badań Młodzieży ISNS UW.

Feldman, R.M. & Stall, S. (1994). "The Politics of Space Appropriation: A Case Study of Women's Struggles for Homeplace in Chicago Public Housing". In I. Altman & A. Churchman (eds.), *Women and the Environment*, New York: Plenum Press.

Fischer, C.S. (1975). "Toward a Subcultural Theory of Urbanism". *American Journal of Sociology*, 80(6), 1319–1341.

Fischer, C.S. (1995). "The Subcultural Theory of Urbanism: A Twentieth-Year Assessment". *American Journal of Sociology*, 101(3), 543–577.

Florida, R. (2005). *Cities and the creative class*. London-New York: Routledge.

Florida, R. L. (2002). *The rise of the creative class: and how it's transforming work, leisure, community and everyday life*. New York: Basic books.

Foucault, M. (1975). *Discipline and Punish: the Birth of the Prison*. New York: Random House.

Foucault, M. (1978). *The history of sexuality. Volume 1*. New York, NY: Pantheon.

Foucault, M. (2011). "Film in popular memory: An Interview with Michel Foucault". In J. Olick, V. Vinitzky-Seroussi & D.Levy (eds.), *The Collective Memory Reader*, Oxford: Oxford University Press.

Fronczyk, A. & Łada, A. (2009). "Niemcy i polityka europejska w oczach Polaków". In L. Kolarska-Bobińska & A. Łada (eds.), *Polska–Niemcy. Wzajemny wizerunek i wizja Europy*, Warsaw: Instytut Spraw Publicznych.

Frydrych, W. (2002). *Żywoty mężów pomarańczowych*, Wrocław: Pomarańczowa Alternatywa.

Gabiś, A. (2011). "Osiedla po II wojnie światowej". In *Leksykon architektury Wrocławia*, Wrocław: Via Nova.

Gedi, N. & Elam, Y. (1996). "Collective Memory—What Is It?". *History and memory*, 8(1), 30–50.

Gelder, K. (2007). *Subcultures. Cultural histories and Social Practice*. London-New York: Routledge.

Giddens, A. (1984). *The Constitution of Society: Outline of the Theory of Structuration*. Oxford: Polity Press.

Glaeser, E. (2011). *Triumph of the city: How our greatest invention makes us richer, smarter, greener, healthier, and happier*. New York: Penguin Press.

Glaeser, E. L. & Gottlieb, J. D. (2006). "Urban resurgence and the consumer city". *Urban studies*, 43(8), 1275–1299.

Glaeser, E. L., Kolko, J., & Saiz, A. (2004). "Consumers and cities". In T.N. Clark (ed.), *The City as an Entertainment Machine*, Bingley: Emerald.

Golka, M. (2009). *Pamięć społeczna i jej implanty*. Warsaw: Scholar.

Goodwin, N.R., Ackerman, F., & Kiron, D. (1997). *The Consumer Society*. Washington D.C.: Island Press.

Gramsci, A. (1968). *Prison Notebook*. London: Lawrence and Wishart.

Grębowiec, J. (2008). *Inskrypcje w przestrzeni otwartej Wrocławia*. Wrocław: Atut.

Gregorowicz, R. & Waloch, J. (1991). *Polskie mury: graffiti – sztuka czy wandalizm.* Torun: Comer.

Grubb, E. L., & Grathwohl, H. L. (1967). "Consumer self-concept, symbolism and market behavior: A theoretical approach". *The Journal of Marketing*, 22–27.

Gzell, S. (2009). "Polskie miasto w stanie przejściowym: między zwartością a rozproszeniem". In I. Jażdżewska (ed.), *Duże i średnie miasta polskie w okresie transformacji*, Łódź: Wyd. UŁ.

Haferburg, C. (2011). "South Africa under FIFA's reign: The World Cup's contribution to urban development". *Development Southern Africa*, 28(3), 333–348.

Hagedorn, J. M. (2007). "Gangs, Institutions, Race and Space: The Chicago School Revisited". In J.M. Hagedorn (ed.), *Gangs in the Global City: Alternatives to Traditional Criminology*, Chicago: University of Illinois.

Halbwachs, M. (1992). *On Collective Memory.* Chicago-London: The University of Chicago Press.

Harrison, L.A., & Huntington, S.P. (2000). *Kultura ma znaczenie: jak wartości wpływają na rozwój społeczeństw*, transl. S. Dymczyk. Poznan: Zysk i S-ka.

Harvey, D. (1987). "Flexible accumulation through urbanization: reflections on 'post-modernism'in the American city". *Antipode*, 19(3), 260–286.

Harvey, D. (2008). "The right to the city". *The City Reader*, 6, 23–40.

Harvey, D. (2012). *Rebel Cities: From the Right to the City to the Urban Revolution.* London: Verso Books.

Harvey, D. (2012). *Rebel cities: From the right to the city to the urban revolution.* New York: Verso.

Hausner, J., Karwieńska, A. & Purchla J. (eds.) (2013). *Kultura a rozwój.* Warsaw: Narodowe Centrum Kultury.

Hobsbawm, E. J. (2012). "Introduction: Inventing traditions". In E. Hobsbawm & T. Ranger, *The invention of tradition*, Cambridge: Cambridge University Press.

Hołyst, B. (2007). *Socjologia kryminalistyczna*, Warsaw: Lexis Nexis.

Horton, D. et al. (eds.) (2007). *Cycling and society.* Hampshire: Ashgate Publishing.

Igartua, J., & Paez, D. (1997). "Art and remembering traumatic collective events: The case of the Spanish Civil War". In J. W. Pennebaker, D. Paez, & B. Rim, *Collective memory of political events*, Mahwah, NJ: Lawrence Erlbaum Associates.

Ilczuk, D. & Nowak, M. (2011). "Reforma sektora kultury w Polsce. W czym jest problem?" In B. Jung (ed.), *Ekonomika kultury. Od teorii do praktyki*, Warsaw: Narodowe Centrum Kultury.

Instytut Demoskopii w Allensbach (2011). *Poważny krok w kierunku normalności. Stan stosunków polsko-niemieckich Wyniki reprezentatywnych bada opinii publicznej w Polsce i w Niemczech.* Warsaw: Fundacja Współpracy Polsko-Niemieckiej.

Instytut Spraw Publicznych (2005). *Opinie Polaków o stosunkach polsko-niemieckich po zmianie rządów w obu krajach.* Warsaw.

Instytut Spraw Publicznych (2009). *70 lat później. Jak Polacy oceniają stosunki polsko-niemieckie i niemiecką politykę europejską.* Warsaw

Jałowiecki, B. & Szczepański, M. (2002). *Miasto i przestrzeń w perspektywie socjologicznej.* Warsaw: Scholar.

Jałowiecki, B. (2000). *Społeczna przestrzeń metropolii.* Warsaw: Wydawnictwo Naukowe Scholar.

Jałowiecki, B. (2002). *Reguły działania w społeczeństwie i nauce. Szkice socjologiczne.* Warsaw: Wydawnictwo Naukowe Scholar.

Jałowiecki, B. (2003). "Tożsamość ludzi, tożsamość miejsc". In M. Dymnicka & Z. Opacki (eds.), *Gdańszczanie i ich miasto w perspektywie historyczno – socjologicznej,* Warsaw: Oficyna Naukowa.

Jameson, F. (1991). *Postmodernism, or the cultural logic of late capitalism.* Durham: Duke University Press.

Jarosz, M. (ed.) (2008). *Transformacja. Elity. Społeczeństwo.* Warsaw: IFiS PAN.

Jayne, M. (2005). *Cities and consumption.* London-New York: Routledge.

Jędrzejewski, M. (2001). *Subkultury a przemoc.* Warsaw: Żak.

Johnson, R., & Dawson, G. (1982). "Popular memory: theory, politics, method". in R. Johnson, G. McLennan, B. Schwarz & D. Sutton (eds), *Making Histories: Studies in History Writing and Politics,* London: Hutchinson.

Johnson, R., & Dawson, G. (1998). "Popular memory: theory, politics, method". In R. Perks & T. Alistair (eds), *Oral history Reader,* NY: Routledge.

Jordan, T. (2011). *Hakerstwo.* Warsaw: PWN.

Kaczmar, M. "Dzielnica Wzajemnego Szacunku Czterech Wyznań - jedyna taka w Polsce". *Gazeta Wrocławska,* 18 September 2009.

Kajdanek, K. & Pluta, J. (2016). "Aktywność lokalna a potencjał grup interesu". *Przegląd Socjologiczny,* vol 65, 101–125.

Kajdanek, K. (2011). *Pomiędzy miastem a wsią: suburbanizacja na przykładzie osiedli podmiejskich Wrocławia.* Cracow: Nomos.

Kansteiner, W. (2002). "Finding meaning in memory: A methodological critique of collective memory studies". *History and theory,* 41(2), 179–197.

Kanter, R. M. (2003). "Thriving locally in the global economy". *Harvard Business Review,* 81(8), 119–128.

Karabon, K. & Karabon, M. (2016). *Migawki z diagnozy Wrocławia.* Unpublished material.

Klasik, A. (2009). *Przemysły kreatywne oparte na nauce i kulturze. Kreatywne miasto - kreatywna aglomeracja.* Katowice: Akademia Ekonomiczna w Katowicach.

Klein, M. W. & Maxson, C. L. (2006). *Street Gang Patterns and Policies (Studies in Crime and Public Policy).* Oxford: Oxford University Press.

Kłopot, S.W. (2012). *Wielokulturowe dziedzictwo miasta a polityka historyczna władz samorządowych Wrocławia. Społeczne światy wartości.* Lublin: Wydywnistwo IMCS.

Kolasa-Nowak, A. (1999). "W poszukiwaniu teorii zmiany makrostrukturalnej. Modelująca socjologia historyczna Charlesa Tilly'ego". *Annales Universitatis Mariae Curie-Skłodowska Lublin-Polonia,* 24(1), 11–32.

Kończal, K. and Wawrzyniak, J. (2011). "Polskie badania pamięcioznawcze. Tradycje, koncepcje, (nie) ciągłości". *Kultura i Społeczeństwo,* 55(4), 11–63.

Kościółek, S. (2014). "Efekt nowego stadionu w polskiej Ekstraklasie piłkarskiej w latach 2007–2014". In K. Nessel & E. Wszendybył-Skulska (eds.), *Młodzi o sporcie 2014. Organizacja i marketing imprez sportowych,* Cracow: Katedra Zarządzania w Turystyce Uniwersytetu Jagielońskiego.

Kosiewski, P. & Cichocki, M. (2008). *Pamięć jako przedmiot władzy.* Warsaw: Fundacja im. Stefana Batorego.

Kosiński, L. (1960). "Pochodzenie terytorialne ludności Wrocławia wg. spisu z 1950 roku. Pochodzenie terytorialne ludności Ziem Zachodnich w 1950 roku". *Dokumentacja Geograficzna,* no. 2.

Kowalewski, M. (2013). "Organizowanie miejskiego aktywizmu w Polsce: Kongres Ruchów Miejskich". *Przestrzeń Społeczna (Social Space),* 2(6), 99–124.

Kozdraś, G. (2006). "Subkultury i ich przestrzenie w mieście Wrocławiu. Zawłaszczanie przestrzeni osiedli miejskich przez wybrane subkultury młodzieżowe". In M. Malikowski & S. Solecki, *Przemiany przestrzenne w dużych miastach Polski i Europy Środkowo-Wschodniej,* Cracow: Nomos.

Kozdraś, G. (2011). "Między domem a miastem. Podbój i zawłaszczanie przestrzeni publicznych miast przez subkultury młodzieżowe". *Forum Socjologiczne,* no. 2, 89–105.

Krätke, S. (2012). *The creative capital of cities: interactive knowledge creation and the urbanization economies of innovation.* New York: John Wiley & Sons.

Krier, L. (2011). *Architektura wspólnoty.* Gdańsk: Słowo/Obraz Terytoria.

Kryńska, E. J., & Mauersberg, S. (2003). *Indoktrynacja młodzieży szkolnej w Polsce w latach 1945–1956.* Bialystok: Trans Humana.

Krysiński, D. (2014). "Samochód – początek i koniec mobilności". *Autoportret*, vol. 2, 37–43.

Krzemiński, I. (ed.) (2010). *Wielka transformacja. Zmiany ustroju w Polsce po 1989*. Warsaw: Oficyna Wydawnicza Łośgraf.

Kubicki, P. (2011). *Nowi mieszczanie w nowej Polsce. Raport z badań*. Warsaw: Instytut Obywatelski.

Kubicki, P. (2013). "Polskie ruchy miejskie in statu nascendi". In A. Maszkowska & K. Sztop-Rutkowska (eds.), *Partycypacja obywatelska – decyzje bliższe ludziom*, Bialystok: Fundacja Laboratorium Badań i Działań Społecznych "SocLab".

Łada, A. (2010). *20 lat później. Polacy o stosunkach polsko-niemieckich i niemieckiej polityce europejskiej w 20 lat po zjednoczeniu Niemiec*. Warsaw: Instytut Spraw Publicznych.

Łada, A. (2011). *Patrzymy w przyszłość. Polacy o polsko-niemieckiej współpracy i o znaczeniu historii we wzajemnych stosunkach*. Warsaw: Instytut Spraw Publicznych.

Lalewicz, J. (1975). *Komunikacja językowa i literatura*. Wrocław: Zakład Narodowy im. Ossolińskich.

Lalewicz, J. (1985). *Socjologia komunikacji literackiej. Problemy rozpowszechniania i odbioru literatury*. Wrocław: Ossolineum.

Lefebvre, H. (1990). *The Production of space*. Oxford: Blackwell.

Lewandowski, C. (1993). *Kierunki tak zwanej ofensywy ideologicznej w polskiej oświacie, nauce i szkołach wyższych, w latach 1944–1948 (Vol. 34)*. Wrocław: Wydawnictwo Uniwersytetu Wrocławskiego.

Lewis, K., Gray, K. & Meierhenrich, J. (2014). "The Structure of Online Activism", *Sociological Science*, 1, 1–9.

Litorowicz, A. (2012). *Subkultura hispsterów. Od nowoczesnej etyki do postnowoczesnej estetyki*. Warsaw: Katedra Wydawnictwo Naukowe.

Lorens, P. (2007). "Tematyzacja przestrzeni publicznej jako wyraz dywersyfikacji struktury urbanistycznej miasta doby globalizacji". In M. Madurowicz (ed.) *Percepcja przestrzeni miejskiej*, Warsaw: Wyd. WGiSR UW.

Majer, A. (2010). *Socjologia i przestrzeń miejska*. Warsaw: PWN.

Majer, A. (2014). *Odrodzenie Miast*. Warszawa: Wydawnictwo Naukowe Scholar.

Martinez-Fernandez, C., et al. (2012). "Shrinking cities: Urban challenges of globalization". *International Journal of Urban and Regional Research*, 36(2), 213–225.

Mazur, Z. (1995). *Obraz Niemiec w polskich podręcznikach szkolnych do nauczania historii: 1945–1989 (Vol. 62)*. Poznań: Instytut Zachodni.

McAdam, D. (1982). "The political process model". In Idem, *Political process and development of Black Insurgency*, Chcicago: University of Chicago Press.

McAdam, D. (2008). "Model procesu politycznego". In K. Gorlach and P. H. Mooney (eds.), *Dynamika życia społecznego. Współczesne koncepcje ruchów społecznych*, Warsaw: Scholar.

Meusburger, P. (2015). "Relations between knowledge and power: An overview of research questions and concepts". In P. Meusburger, D. Gregory, & L. Suarsana, (eds.), *Geographies of knowledge and power*, Dordrecht: Springer.

Miecik I. (2001). "Spacer po żylecie. Chuligani dobrze się bawią bez futbolu". *Polityka*, no. 25.

Ministerstwo Infrastruktury (2006). *Polityka Transportowa Państwa na lata 2006–2025*. Warsaw.

Misztal, B. (2006). *Theories of Social Remembering*. London: Open University Press.

Mooney, P. H. & Hunt Scott, A. (1996). "A repertoire of interpretations: Master frames and ideological continuity in U.S. Agrarian mobilization". *Sociological Quaterly*, 37(1), 177–197.

Mouffe, Ch. (2005). *On the political*. New York: Psychology Press.

Mucha, J. (1999). "Dominacja kulturowa i reakcje na nią". In Idem, (ed.), *Kultura dominująca jako kultura obca. Mniejszości kulturowe a grupa dominująca w Polsce*, Warsaw: Oficyna Naukowa.

Muggleton, D. (2004). *Wewnątrz subkultury. Ponowoczesne znaczenie stylu*. Cracow: UJ.

Muller, J.W. (2004). *Memory and Power in Post-War Europe Studies in the Presence of the Past*. Oxford: Cambridge University Press.

Najwyższa Izba Kontroli (2010). *Informacja o wynikach kontroli działań podejmowanych na rzecz usprawnienia systemu transportowego w największych miastach w Polsce*. Warsaw: 2010.

Nawratek, K. (2005). *Ideologie w przestrzeni, próby demistyfikacji*. Cracow: Universitas.

Nora, P. (2009). "Między pamięcią a historią: *Les Linux de Mémoire*". In A. Leśniak & M. Ziółkowska (eds.), *Tytuł roboczy: archiwum*, Łódź: Muzeum Sztuki w Łodzi.

Norberg-Schulz, Ch. (1971). *Existence, Space and Architecture*. London: Praeger.

Norcliffe, G. (2001). *The Ride to Modernity: The Bicycle in Canada, 1869–1900*. Toronto: University of Toronto Press.

Nowak, J. (2011). *Społeczne reguły pamiętania. Antropologia pamięci zbiorowej*. Cracow: Nomos.

Nowak, S. (1979). "System wartości społeczeństwa polskiego". *Studia Socjologiczne*, 75(4), 155–173.

Nowak, S. (1981). "Values and Attitudes of Polish People". *Scientific American*, 245(1), 45–53.

Nowinowski, S.M., Pomorski, J., & Stobiecki R. (eds.) (2008). *Pamięć i polityka historyczna. Doświadczenia Polski i jej sąsiadów*. Łódź: Instytut Pamięci Narodowej.

Nugroho, Y. & Syarief, S.S. (2012). *Beyond click-activism? New media and political processes in contemporary Indonesia*. Jakarta: Friedrich-Ebert-Stiftung.

Olick, J. K. (1999). "Collective memory: The two cultures". *Sociological theory*, 17(3), 333–348.

Olick, J. K. (2007). "Collective memory and nonpublic opinion: A historical note on a methodological controversy about a political problem". *Symbolic Interaction*, 30(1), 41–55.

Olick, J., Vinitzky-Seroussi, V., & Levy, D. (2011). *The Collective Memory Reader*. Oxford: Oxford University Press.

Orwell, G. (1977). *Nineteen Eighty-Four*. New York: Signet Classics.

Osiński, Z. (2010). "Edukacja historyczna okresu PRL w służbie władzy i ideologii-konsekwencje i zagrożenia". In E. Gorloff, R. Grzybowski, & A. Kołakowski (eds.), *Edukacja w warunkach zniewolenia i autonomii (1945–2009)*, Cracow: Impuls.

Paleczny, T. (1993). "Grupy subkultury młodzieżowej. Próba analizy – propozycje teoretyczne". *Kultura i społeczeństwo*, no 3., 179–190.

Parsons, T. (2013). *Social system*. London-New York: Routledge.

Paszkowski, Z. (2011). *Miasto idealne w perspektywie europejskiej i jego związki z urbanistyką współczesną*. Cracow: Universitas.

Pęczak, M. (1988). "Kilka uwag o trzech obiegach". *Więź*, no 2, 35–47.

Pęczak, M. (1991). "Alternatywne komunikowanie". In J. Wertenstein-Żuławski & M. Pęczak (eds.), *Spontaniczna kultura młodzieżowa*, Wrocław: Wiedza o kulturze.

Pęczak, M. (1992). *Mały słownik subkultur młodzieżowych*. Warsaw: Semper. Pennebaker, J.W. (ed.). *Collective memory of political events: Social psychological perspectives*. Mahwah, N.J.: Lawrence Erlbaum Associates.

Pęczak, M. (2013). *Subkultury w PRL: opór, kreacja, imitacji*. Warsaw: NCK.

Pennebaker, J.W. (ed.). *Collective memory of political events: Social psychological perspectives*. Mahwah, N.J.: Lawrence Erlbaum Associates.

Petrova, Y. (2006). "Multi-level identifications among contemporary skinheads in France". In P. Nilan & C. Feixa (eds.), *Global Youth? Hibrid Identities, Plural Worlds*, London-New York: Routledge.

Pickvance, C. (1985). "The rise and fall or urban movements and the role of comparative Analysis". *Environment and Planning D: Society and Space*, 3(1), 31–53.

Pickvance, C. (2003). "From urban social movements to urban movements: a review and introduction to a symposium on urban movements". *International Journal of Urban and Regional Research*, 27(1), 102–109.

Piotrowski, P. (2003). *Subkultury młodzieżowe. Aspekty psychospołeczne*. Warsaw: Żak.

Pluciński, P. (2013). "Miejskie (r)ewolucje. Radykalizm retoryki a praktyka reformy". *Praktyka Teoretyczna*, 9(3), 133–157.

Prus, R. (2006). *Subcultural Mosaics and Intersubjective Realities: An Ethnographic research agenda for pragmatizing the social sciences*. Albany, NY: State University of New York Press.

Radstone, S. (2000). *Memory and Methodology*. NewYork; Berg.

Radstone, S. (2008). "Memory studies: For and against". *Memory Studies*, 1(1), 31–39.

Ranger, T. (2012). "The invention of Tradition in Colonial Africa". In E. Hobsbawm, & T. Ranger (eds.) *The invention of tradition*, Cambridge: Cambridge University Press.

Ranger, T. (1993). "The Invention of Tradition Revisited: The Case of Colonial Africa". In T. Ranger & O. Vaughan, *Legitimacy and the State in Twentieth-century Africa*, London: Macmillan.

Richards, G., & Palmer, R. (2010). *Eventful Cities: Cultural Management and Urban Regeneration*. Oxford: Butterworth-Heinemann.

Roediger, H. L., & Wertsch, J. V. (2008a). "Creating a new discipline of memory studies". *Memory Studies*, 1(1), 9–22.

Rogerson, R. J., Findlay, A. M., Paddison, R., & Morris, A. S. (1996). "Class, consumption and quality of life". *Progress in Planning*, 1(45), 1–66.

Rosenzweig, R., & Thelen, D. P. (1998). *The presence of the past: Popular uses of history in American life (Vol. 2)*. New York: Columbia University Press.

Sahaj, T. (2012). "Aktywność stadionowa kibicowskich grup *ultras* jako przejaw specyficznej komunikacji społecznej". *Kultura i Społeczeństwo*, 56(3), 3–23.

Saryusz-Wolska, M. (2011). "O źródłach pamięci miasta w nowoczesności". *Kultura i Społeczeństwo*, no 55(4), 93–105.

Saryusz-Wolska, M. (2014). "Pamięć kulturowa". In M. Saryusz Wolska & R. Traba, *Mondi memoranda. Leksykon kultury pamięci*, Warsaw: Scholar.

Saunders, P. (1979). *Urban politics: a sociological approach*. London: Hutchinson.

Savitch, H. V., & Kantor, P. (2002). *Cities in the international marketplace. The Political Economy of Urban Development in North America and Western Europe*. Princeton, NJ.: Princeton University Press.

Schmidt, F., & Skowrońska, M. (2012). "Goście jadą! Narracje o Euro 2012 w Poznaniu". *Czas Kultury,* 166(1), 12–27.

Schudson, M. (1989). "The Present in the Past versus the Past in the Present". *Communication*, 11(2), 105–113.

Schudson, M. (1993). *Watergate in American memory. How we Remember, forget an reconstruct the past*. New York: Basic Books.

Schudson, M. (2000). *The Power of News*. Cambridge: Harvard University Press.

Schuman, H., & Corning, A. (2016). "The Conversion of Generational Effects into Collective Memories". *International Journal of Public Opinion Research*, edw012.

Schuman, H., & Scott, J. (1989). "Generations and collective memories". *American Sociological Review*, 54(3), 359–381.

Schuman, H., Belli, R.F. & Bischoping, K. (1997). "The generational basis of historical knowledge". In J.W. Pennebaker, D. Paez & B. Rime (eds.), *Collective Memory of Political Events*, Mahwah, NJ: Lawrence Erlbaum.

Scott, A. J. (2007). "Capitalism and Urbanization in a New Key? The Cognitive-Cultural Dimension". *Social Forces*, 85(4), 1465–1482.

Scott, A. J. (2008). *Social Economy of the Metropolis: Cognitive-Cultural Capitalism and the Global Resurgence of Cities: Cognitive-Cultural Capitalism and the Global Resurgence of Cities*. Oxford: Oxford University Press.

Segal, R. (2004). *Myth. A very short introduction*. Oxford: Oxford University Press.

Sennett, R. (2011). "Disturbing memories". In J. Olick, V. Vinitzky-Seroussi, & D.Levy, *The Collective Memory Reader*, Oxford: Oxford University Press.

Sennett, R. (2006). *The culture of the new capitalism*. New Haven-London: Yale University Press.

Shearmur, R. (2006). "The new knowledge aristocracy: the creative class, mobility and urban growth". *Work Organisation, Labour and Globalisation*, 1(1), 31–47.

Sheller, M. & Urry, J. (2000). "The City and the Car". *International Journal of Urban and Regional Research*, 24(4), 737–757.

Siemaszko, A. (1993). *Granice tolerancji. O teoriach zachowań dewiacyjnych*. Warsaw: PWN.

Silver, D., & Nichols Clark, T. (2015). "The power of scenes: quantities of amenities and qualities of places". *Cultural Studies*, 29(3), 425–449.

Silver, D., Clark, T. N., & Yanez, C. J. N. (2010). "Scenes: Social context in an age of contingency". *Social Forces*, 88(5), 2293–2324.

Skorupka, D., & Górski, M. (2010). "Rozwój infrastruktury Wrocławia w świetle przygotowań do Piłkarskich Mistrzostw Europy EURO 2012". *Czasopismo Techniczne. Budownictwo*, 107(2), 365–377.

Smith, M. K., & Richards, G. (2013). *The Routledge handbook of cultural tourism*. London-New York: Routledge.

Smoleń, M. (2003a). "Przemysły kultury – ekonomiczny wymiar sektora kultury". *Zarządzanie kulturą*, vol. 4, 61–71.

Smoleń, M., (2003b). *Przemysły kultury i wpływ na rozwój miast*. Cracow: Wydawnictwo Uniwersytetu Jagiellońskiego.

Środa-Murawska, S., & Szymańska, D. (2013). "Przemysły kultury a rozwój miast. Wybrane aspekty". *Zeszyty Naukowe Uniwersytetu Szczecińskiego, Ekonomiczne Problemy Usług*, no. 107, 85–98.

Storper, M., & Manville, M. (2006). "Behaviour, preferences and cities: Urban theory and urban resurgence". *Urban studies*, 43(8), 1247–1274.

Sugrue, T. J. (1996). *The Origins of the Urban Crisis: Race and Inequality in Postwar Detroit: Race and Inequality in Postwar Detroit*. Princeton, NJ.: Princeton University Press.

Sułek, A. (2013). "Doświadczenie, działania dla społeczności i kompetencje obywatelskie". *Contemporary Economics*, 7(3.1), 275–284.

Supruniuk, A. and Supruniuk, M.A. (2015). *Drugi obieg wydawniczy (1974) 1976–1990 w zasobie Biblioteki Uniwersyteckiej w Toruniu*. Warsaw: IPN.

Świrek, K. (2012). "Ideologie dobrze ugruntowane: klasowe wizje przestrzeni społecznej". In M. Gdula & P. Sadura (eds.), *Style życia i porządek klasowy w Polsce*, Warsaw: Scholar.

Szacka, B. (2006). *Czas przeszły, pamięć, mit*. Warsaw: Wydawnictwo Naukowe Scholar.

Szawiel, T. (1982). "Struktura społeczna i postawy a grupy etosowe". *Studia socjologiczne*, 1–2(84–85), 157–178.

Szlendak, T. (2010). "Wielozmysłowa kultura iwentu. Skąd się wzięła, czym się objawia i jak w jej ramach oceniać dobra kultury?". *Kultura Współczesna*, 2010, 4(66), 229–257.

Theiss, A. (2012). "Kultura: koło zamachowe zamiast fajerwerków. Z Philippem Kernem rozmawia Anna Theiss". In B. Jung (ed.), *Ekonomika Kultury. Od teorii do praktyki*, Warsaw: Narodowe Centrum Kultury.

Thorsby, D. (2010). *Ekonomia i kultura*, transl. O. Siara. Warsaw: Narodowe Centrum Kultury.

Thum, G. (2008). *Obce miasto Wrocław 1945 i potem*. Wrocław: Wydawnictwo Via Nova.

Tilly, C. (1978). *From mobilization to Revolution*. Reading: Addison-Wesley.

Toffler, A. (1981). *The third wave*. New York: Bantam Books.

Touraine, A. (1981). *The Voice and the Eye. An analysis of social movements*. Cambridge: Cambridge University Press.

Touraine, A. (2009). *Thinking differently*, translated by David Macey. Cambridge: Polity Press.

Touraine, A. (2013). *La fin des sociétés*. Paris: Seuil.

Towse, R. (2011). *Ekonomia kultury. Kompendium*, transl. H. Dębowski, K.L. Pogorzelski, & Ł.M. Skrok. Warsaw: Narodowe Centrum Kultury.

Urbanik, J. (2009). *WUWA 2009. Wrocławska wystawa Werkbundu*. Wrocław: Muzeum Architektury.

Van Aelst, P. & Walgraave, S. (2004). "New media, new movements? The role of the internet in shaping the 'anti-globalization' movement". In W. van de Donk, et al. (eds.), *Cyberprotest: new media, citizens and social movements*, London: Routledge.

Vinitzky-Seroussi, V. (2002). "Commemoration a difficult past: Yitzhak Rabin's Memorials". *American Sociological Review*, 67(1), 30–51.

Wallis, A. (1977). *Miasto i przestrzeń*. Warsaw: PWN.

Wallis, A. (1979). *Informacja i gwar. O miejskim centrum*. Warsaw: PIW.

Wattanasuwan, K. (2005). "The self and symbolic consumption". *Journal of American Academy of Business*, 6(1), 179–184.

Wehler, H.U. (1998). *Die Herausforderung der Kulturgeschichte*. Munich: Achims Verlag.

Wertenstein-Żuławski, J. (1990). *To tylko rock'n roll!*. Warsaw: ZAKR.

Wertenstein-Żuławski, J. (1991). "Trzy obiegi – trzy kultury. Struktura społeczna i komunikowanie w dzisiejszej Polsce". In A. Sułek A & W. Wincławski (eds.), *Przełom i wyzwanie. Pamiętniki VIII Ogólnopolskiego Zjazdu Socjologicznego. Toruń 19–22 września 1990*, Warsaw-Torun: Wydawnictwo Adam Marszałek.

Wertsch, J. V. (2004). "Specific narratives and schematic narrative templates". In P. Seixas (ed.), *Theorizing historical consciousness*, Toronto: University of Toronto Press.

Wertsch, J. V., & Roediger III, H. L. (2008b). "Collective memory: Conceptual foundations and theoretical approaches". *Memory*, 16(3), 318–326.

White, R. (1985). "Demokratyzacja komunikowania. W poszukiwaniu nowych strategii badawczych". *Przekazy i Opinie*, no. 3–4, 31–62.

Whitehead, A., & Rossington, M. (2007). *Theories of Memory. A Reader.* Edinburgh: Edinburgh University Press.

Wnuk-Lipiński, E. & Ziółkowski, M. (2001). *Pierwsza dekada niepodległości. Próba socjologicznej syntezy.* Warsaw: ISP PAN.

Wrzesień, W. (2003). *Jednostka – rodzina – pokolenie: studum relacji międzypokoleniowych w rodzinie.* Poznań: Wyd. Naukowe UAM.

Wrzesień, W. (2013). *Krótka historia młodzieżowej subkulturowości.* Warsaw: PWN.

Wynne, D. & O'Connor, J. (1998). "Consumption and the postmodern city". *Urban Studies,* 35(5/6), 841–864.

Ziółkowski, M. (1999). "O imitacyjnej modernizacji społeczeństwa polskiego". In P. Sztompka (ed.), *Imponderabilia okresu wielkiej zmiany. Mentalność, wartości i więzi społeczne czasów transformacji,* Warsaw-Cracow: PWN.

Ziółkowski, M. (2001). "Pamięć i zapominanie: trupy w szafie polskiej zbiorowej pamięci". *Kultura i Społeczeństwo,* 45(3–4), 3–22.

Zukin, S. (1993). *Landscapes of power: from Detroit to Disney World.* Berkeley: University of California Press.

Zukin, S. (1998). "Urban lifestyles: diversity and standardisation in spaces of consumption". *Urban studies,* 35(5–6), 825–839.

Zukin, S. (2010). *Naked City: The Death and Life of Authentic Urban Places.* New York: Oxford University Press.

Electronic database

Beim, M. (2011) *Sprawny transport publiczny w polskich miastach.* Warsaw: Instytut Sobieskiego. Available at: http://www.sobieski.org.pl/wp-content/uploads/Raport_IS_nr_40-beim_transpory_2011.pdf [Accessed 18 April 2015].

Borejza, T. (2015): "Ruchy miejskie to nie jest partia polityczna". Available at: http://krowoderska.pl/ruchy-miejskie-nie-jest-partia-polityczna/ [Accessed 28 June 2015].

Brzozowski, A. "Konsorcjum nie kupi piłkarskiego Śląska? Wrocław może mieć problem". Available at: http://wroclaw.wyborcza.pl/wroclaw/1,35771,19246305,konsorcjum-nie-kupi-pilkarskiego-slaska-wroclaw-moze-miec-problem.html [Accessed 11 February 2016].

Brzozowski, A. "Wrocław przejmuje Śląsk: Ambitne plany miasta". Available at: http://www.sport.pl/sport/1,67926,3645870.html [Accessed 29 January 2016].

Brzozowski, A. "Wrocław zasługuje na porządny klub piłkarski". Available at: http://www.wroclaw.sport.pl/sport-wroclaw/1,123437,6693347,Wrocław_zasluguje_na_porzadny_klub_pilkarski.html [Accessed 30 January 2016].

Czapiński, J. & Panek, T. (eds.) (2013). *Diagnoza Społeczna 2013. Warunki i jakość życia Polaków*, Warsaw: Rada monitoringu społecznego. Available at: http://www.diagnoza.com [Accessed 21 July 2015].

"Dzieci na stadionie – uczymy się dopingu". Available at: http://www.wroclaw.pl/dzieci-na-stadionie-uczymy-sie-dopingu [Accessed 11 February 2016].

Filiciak, M., Hofmokl, J. & Tarkowski, A. (2012). *Obiegi kultury. Społeczna cyrkulacja treści*. Available at: http://obiegikultury.centrumcyfrowe.pl/raport_obiegi_kultury.pdf [Accessed 22 September 2015].

Głowacka, E. "Optymiści znad Odry". Available at: http://wroclaw.naszemiasto.pl/archiwum/optymisci-znad-odry,1195548,art,t,id,tm.html [Accessed 29 September 2016].

Głowacki, J., Hausner, J., Jakóbik, K., Markiel, K., Mituś, A., & Żabiński, M. *Finansowanie kultury i zarządzanie instytucjami kultury*. Available at: www.kongreskultury.pl/library/File/RoSK%20finansowanie_w.pelna.pdf, page 7. [Accessed 10 June 2015].

Główny Urząd Statystyczny (2015). *Polska 1989–2014*. Available at: http://stat.gov.pl/obszary-tematyczne/inne-opracowania/inne-opracowania-zbiorcze/polska-19892014,13,1.html [Accessed 20 July 2015].

Gulder, J. "Oświadczenie Wrocławskiego Konsorcjum Sportowego: Wrocław tylko markował sprzedaż akcji". Available at: http://www.gazetawroclawska.pl/sport/pilka-nozna/slask-wroclaw/a/oswiadczenie-wroclawskiego-konsorcjum-sportowego-wroclaw-tylko-markowal-sprzedaz-akcji,9879493/ [30 April 2016].

Harkułowicz, J. "Pożyczka Śląska Wrocław z naszych rachunków za wodę". Available at: http://wroclaw.wyborcza.pl/wroclaw/1,36743,13897467,Pozyczka_dla_Slaska_Wroclaw_z_naszych_rachunkow_za.html [Accessed 11 February 2016].

Hipsz N., Feliksiak M. (2014). "Polacy o stanie środowiska i zmianach klimatu". Available: http://www.cbos.pl/SPISKOM.POL/2014/K_171_14.PDF [Accessed 22 July 2015].

http://www.transfermarkt.de/slask-wroclaw/besucherzahlenentwicklung/verein/759 [Accessed 11 February 2016].

http://www.tvn24.pl/wroclaw,44/ile-stracil-wroclaw-na-meczu-japonia-brazylia,283223.html [Accessed 11 February 2016].

Karbowiak, M. "Turniej Polish Masters we Wrocławiu był finansową klapą". Available at: http://wroclaw.wyborcza.pl/wroclaw/1,35771,12215816,Turniej_Polish_Masters_we_Wroclawiu_byl_finansowa.html [Accessed 11 February 2016].

Kondrat, M. "#WszyscyZaŚląskiem – zobacz kto nas wspiera i dołącz!" Available at: http://slaskwroclaw.pl/strona/aktualnosci/wszyscyzaslaskiem-zobacz-kto-nas-wspiera-i-dolacz-12836533 [Accessed 11 February 2016].

Kozioł, M. "Wiceprezydent Wrocławia zaprasza dzieci na mecz Brazylia-Japonia. Ale za pieniądze". Available at: http://www.gazetawroclawska.pl/artykul/656245,wiceprezydent-wroclawia-zaprasza-dzieci-na-mecz-brazylia-japonia-ale-za-pieniadze,id,t.html [Accessed 10 February 2016].

Krajowa Polityka Miejska 2014. Available at: http://www.mir.gov.pl/rozwoj_regionalny/polityka_regionalna/rozwoj_miast/kpm/strony/start.aspx; [Accessed 10 May 2015]

Kubicki, P. (2012). "Bunt miast a sprawa polska". Avaliable at: http://www.instytutobywatelski.pl/9022/akcje-instytutu/%E2%80%9Ebunt-miast-a-sprawa-polska [Accessed 16 July 2015].

Lefebvre, H. (2012). "Prawo do miasta". *Praktyka Teoretyczna* no. 5. Availiable at: http:// www.praktykateoretyczna.pl/PT_nr5_2012_Logika_sensu/14.Lefebvre.pdf [Accessed 17 July 2015].

Lenkowski, B. (2014). "Ruchy miejskie – spojrzenie z dystansu". Avaliable at: http://www.instytutobywatelski.pl/22225/lupa-instytutu/ruchy-miejskie-spojrzenie-z-dystansu [Accessed 6 July 2015].

Markusen, A. *Urban Development and the Politics of a Creative Class: Evidence from the Study of Artists.* Available at: http://www.hhh.umn.Edu/projects/prie/pdf/266_creativity_class_politics.pdf [Accessed 25 May 2015].

NIK Delegatura w Warszawie (2010). *Informacja o wynikach kontroli działań podejmowanych na rzecz usprawnienia systemu transportowego w największych miastach w Polsce, Nr ewid. 4/2010/P/09/178/LWA LWA/41020/09.* [Online] Available at: https://www.nik.gov.pl/plik/id,1816,vp,2122.pdf [Accessed 3 March 2015].

Nowaczyk, M. "Jak Wrocław grał na Rynku o Expo 2012". Available at: http://wroclaw.wyborcza.pl/wroclaw/1,35771,4235159.html [Accessed 29 January 2016].

Pabjan, B. & Czajkowski, P. (2015). "Symbole w pamięci zbiorowej Wrocławia: pomniki jako wehikuł lokalnej pamięci historyczno-kulturowej". Available at: http://www.academia.edu/9428063/Symbole_w_pami%C4%99ci_zbiorowej_Wroc%C5%82awia_pomniki_jako_wehiku%C5%82_lokalnej_pami%C4%99ci_historyczno-kulturowej [Accessed 28 September 2015].

"Piłkarze Śląska spotkali się w tym roku z pięcioma tysiącami uczniów". Available at: http://www.wroclaw.sport.pl/sport-wroclaw/1,123437,13088414,Pilkarze_Slaska_spotkali_sie_w_tym_roku_z_pieciacma.html [Accessed 11 February 2016].

Pluta, P. "Mecz Brazylia-Japonia przyniósł straty. To koniec piłkarskich gwiazd we Wrocławiu?" Available at: http://www.gazetawroclawska.pl/artykul/683709, mecz-brazyliajaponia-przyniosl-straty-to-koniec-pilkarskich-gwiazd-we-wroclawiu,id,t.html [Accessed 11 February 2016].

Rybak, M. & Torz, M., "AFERA STADIONOWA: Gdzie jest 14 mln zł po koncercie Queen i turnieju Polish Masters?". Available at: http://www.gazetawroclawska. pl/artykul/668949,afera-stadionowa-gdzie-jest-14-mln-zl-po-koncercie-queen-i-turnieju-polish-masters,id,t.html, [accessed 11 February 2016].

Schwartz, M. L. (2010). "Cycling as a political act: the framing and culture that create a new social movement". Master's Thesis, University of Kentucky. Avaliable at: http://uknowledge.uky.edu/gradschool_theses/6 [Accessed 16 April 2015].

Scott, A. J. *Beyond the Creative City: Cognitive – Cultural Capitalism and the New Urbanism*. Available at: www.academia.edu/6444858/Beyond_the_creative_city_cognitive-cultural_capitalism_and_the_new_urbanism [Accessed 11 May 2015].

Skrzyński, R. "Promocja maratonu? Nie, pompowanie kasy w Śląsk". Radio programme. Available at: http://www.radiowroclaw.pl/articles/view/36768/Jak-Slask-maraton-promowal-Za-milion-zlotych [Accessed 11 February 2016].

Staszak, J. "Pusto jak we Wrocławiu. Czy Śląsk jeszcze kogoś obchodzi?". Available at: http://www.sport.pl/pilka/1,65039,19111619,ekstraklasa-w-sport-pl-pusto-jak-we-wroclawiu-czy-slask-jeszcze.html [Accessed 11 February 2016].

Szlendak, T. (2010). "Samochód to dla Polaka emanacja jakiejś boskości". Available at: http://warszawa.gazeta.pl/warszawa/1,90134,8721288,_Samochod_to_dla_Polaka_emanacja_jakiejs_boskosci_.html [Accessed 10 May 2015].

"Tauron rozstaje się ze Śląskiem Wrocław". Available at: http://sport.wp.pl/kat, 98810,title,Tauron-rozstaje-sie-ze-Slaskiem-Wroclaw,wid,17127247, wiadomosc.html, [Accessed 11 February 2016].

Torz, M. (2010). "Śląsk Wrocław: Kibice sławią swój klub na murach". Available at: http://www.gazetawroclawska.pl/artykul/290565,slask-wroclaw-kibice-slawia-zespol-na-murach,id,t.html?cookie=1 [Accessed 22 September 2015].

Wiersztot, A. & Kocinia, A. (2015). "Wkurzeni mieszczanie". Available at: http://beczmiana.pl/646,wkurzeni_mieszczanie.html [Accessed 14 July 2015].

"Władze miasta odpierają zarzuty konsorcjum w sprawie Śląska". Aailable at: http://www.gazetawroclawska.pl/sport/pilka-nozna/slask-wroclaw/a/wladze-miasta-odpieraja-zarzuty-konsorcjum-w-sprawie-slaska,9886043/ [Accessed 30 April 2016].

Wolski, Ł. "Miasto w tajemnicy finansuje piłkarski Śląsk. Kto za to płaci? My płacimy". Available at: http://wdolnymslasku.pl/wydarzenia/900-miasto-w-tajemnicy-finansuje-pilkarski-slask-kto-za-to-placi-my-placimy [Accessed 28 February 2016].

Wróbewski M., Dobroszek K. (2014). *Makowski: w Polsce następuje odrodzenie mieszczaństwa. Jego symbolem są ruchy miejskie.* "Polska Times". Available at: http://www.polskatimes.pl/artykul/3682608,makowski-w-polsce-nastepuje-odrodzenie-mieszczanstwa-jego-symbolem-sa-ruchy-miejskie,2,id,t,sa.html [Accessed 23 February 2017].

Wróblewski, M. & Dobroszek, K. (2014). "Makowski: W Polsce następuje odrodzenie mieszczaństwa. Jego symbolem są ruchy miejskie". Available at: http://www.polskatimes.pl/artykul/3682608,makowski-w-polsce-nastepuje-odrodzenie-mieszczanstwa-jego-symbolem-sa-ruchy-miejskie,3,id,t,sa.html [Accessed 16 July 2015].

"Wrocław znów stara się o Expo". Radio programme. Available at: *http://*www.rmf24.pl/fakty/polska/news-wrclaw-znow-stara-sie-o-expo,nId,80231. [Accessed 10 February 2016].

Sources of German statistical data

Knie, J.G. (1830). *Alphabetisch-Statistisch-Topographische Uebersicht aller Dörfer, Flecken, Städte und anderen Orte der Königl. Preuß. Provinz Schlesien*, Breslau.

Die Gemeinden un Gutsbezirke des Preussischen Staates und ihre Bevölkerung. Nach den Uhrmaterialen der allgemein Volkszählung vom 1. December 1871 bearbeitet und zusammengeschtellt von Königlischen Statistischen Bureau, Berlin 1874.

Gemeindelexikon für die Provinz Schlesien. Auf Grund der Materialen der Volkszälung vom 1. Dezember 1885 und anderer amtlischer Quellen bearbeitet von Königlischen Statistischen Bureau, Berlin 1887.

Gemeindelexikon für die Provinz Schlesien. Auf Grund der Materialen der Volkszälung vom 2. Dezember 1895 und anderer amtlischer Quellen bearbeitet von Königlischen Statistischen Bureau, Berlin 1898.

Gemeindelexikon für die Provinz Schlesien. Auf Grund der Materialen der Volkszälung vom 1. Dezember 1905 und anderer amtlischer Quellen bearbeitet vom königlisch Preußischen Statistischen Landesamte, Berlin 1908.

Statistische Daten über die Stadt Breslau. Nach amtlische Quellen zusammengestellt, Breslau 1901, 1903, 1904, 1905, 1906, 1907, 1910, 1912, 1913.

Warsaw Studies in Philosophy and Social Sciences

Edited by Tadeusz Szawiel and Jakub Kloc-Konkołowicz

Vol.	1	Paweł Skuczyński: The Status of Legal Ethics. 2013.
Vol.	2	Szymon Wróbel: Grammar and Glamour of Cooperation. Lectures on the Philosophy of Mind, Language and Action. 2014.
Vol.	3	Zbigniew Drozdowicz: Cartesian Rationalism. Understanding Descartes. 2015.
Vol.	4	Daria Lebedeva: Quaternion of the Examples of a Philosophical Influence: Schopenhauer-Dostoevsky-Nietzsche-Cioran. 2015.
Vol.	5	Antal Szerletics: Paternalism. Moral Theory and Legal Practice. 2015.
Vol.	6	Dorota Pietrzyk-Reeves: Civil Society, Democracy and Democratization. 2015.
Vol.	7	Małgorzata Bogunia-Borowska (ed.): Social Spaces and Social Relations. Introduction by Anthony Giddens. 2016.
Vol.	8	Katarzyna Kajdanek/Igor Pietraszewski/Jacek Pluta (eds.): City and Power – Postmodern Urban Spaces in Contemporary Poland. 2018.

www.peterlang.com